# THE SCOTTISH PARISH KIRK

DALMENY, WEST LOTHIAN

A fine interior dating from the 12th century

# THE SCOTTISH PARISH KIRK

### IAN G. LINDSAY
O.B.E., B.A., R.S.A., F.R.I.B.A.

THE SAINT ANDREW PRESS
EDINBURGH

726.50941 ✓

A. 17867.

G. 10602

2 006331

TO
MY WIFE

# ACKNOWLEDGMENTS

MANY people have been most kind and helpful in providing information and making suggestions. To all of these I tender my warmest thanks, but special recognition should be given to Mr. Ronald G. Cant, Mr. Peter F. Anson, Dr. Alice M. Stewart and Mr. George Hay whose *Architecture of Scottish Post Reformation Churches* is the standard work for that period. A word of appreciation must also go to Miss Shirley Hamilton, who produced a readable typescript from most shocking material.

For permission to reproduce photographs I am indebted to the following:

The Royal Commission on the Ancient Monuments of Scotland for plate 4; Mr. George Hay for plates 1, 5, 8, 9 and 14; Mr. W. Schomberg Scott for plates 2 and 6; Messrs. Valentine & Sons Ltd. for plate 11; Messrs. Allan of Glasgow for plate 13; and Sir Basil Spence for plate 15.

Plates 3, 7, 10 and 12 were taken by the author.

# CONTENTS

# ILLUSTRATIONS

# INTRODUCTION

I N a small book such as this it is only possible to
trace a mere outline of the fascinating history of that
misunderstood building, the Scottish parish kirk.
For the last eight hundred years a building in one form
or another has stood as the spiritual centre of each area
of land known as a parish.

No matter what type of service went on within, the
purpose of this building has always been the same and
has been dedicated to the highest use any building could
have. The worship of God together with teaching the
Eternal Truths to the inhabitants of the parish around
has ever been the object of the ceremonies in the parish
kirk. At times the standard of this worship and teaching
may have fallen painfully short of the essential ideal, but
even so the building always stood in the sight of all godly
men as the symbol of their faith.

Consider what the kirk meant to the average parish-
ioner at any time up to the last hundred or hundred-and-
fifty years.

For him there was no shelter open except his kirk;
no institutes, no cinemas, no parish hall, no club. There
was only his own cot house—mean enough no doubt, for
such dwellings could be erected for under £1 as recently
as the 18th century—and God's house. It too may not
have been very grand, but its mere presence in the community must have meant a great deal more than it
can today, and the parish with the kirk as the central

meeting place of its people was a much more important social unit than it is now. It is therefore very necessary to realise how their social unit, the most ancient in our country except the family, came into being so as to understand the function of its central spiritual institution.

To begin with, let us face the fact that most of those who give the parish church, as a building, any second thought are liable to have an 'inferiority complex' about it. It is true that, even proportionally, we do not retain in use anything like the number of ancient medieval churches that other European countries do; but it is equally untrue that the reformers destroyed them.

Few, especially in the country, were the fine buildings we like to imagine, and as the population increased they had to be abandoned to make way for larger and finer kirks suited to the Presbyterian 'use'. Further, though perhaps it is not generally realised, this process of abandoning old kirks still continues and few voices are raised in protest. It is, in fact, rather surprising that so much of our ancient heritage is left after centuries of pressing for the latest type of kirk.

The real story of the parish kirk in Scotland is quite different to the normally accepted tales but, as with so many other things, 'truth is stranger' or, shall we say, more interesting 'than fiction'.

## CHAPTER I

## ROMANESQUE: THE FIRST PARISH KIRKS

THOUGH parishes are now the basic administrative unit of church organisation, their existence by no means dates from the introduction of Christianity to Scotland. Indeed the period covered by the parish system is only rather more than half the time between the founding of St. Ninian's first church at Whithorn in Galloway and our own day. The early saints, Columba, Kentigern, Serf, Machar, Ternan, Blaan, Brandon and others, founded numerous churches and, as in those remote days churches were frequently called after their founder, their sites can often be recognised by place names. This is particularly noticeable in the Highlands where the prefix Kil (from *cille*, a church) gives such names as Kilbride and Kilbrandon. The churches of those days were not, however, parish churches in the present sense, for many were monastic and others were small chapels dependent upon and worked by the monastic communities. In many cases, though, the sites remain as centres of religious life to this day, for most of the medieval cathedrals arose on or near such places, as did a considerable number of parish churches such as Abercorn, Govan and Abernethy. A round tower still stands at Abernethy which, with that at Brechin Cathedral, form the only two considerable architectural relics of Celtic ecclesiastical building in the country.

I

The year 1066, in which the Normans conquered England, does not mark any particular event in this country but the new regime in the south was to have profound influence in Scotland. Among the refugees who came north was Princess Margaret, daughter of Edward the Aetheling. She married the king, Malcolm Canmore, and since she was much occupied with church matters, she was in a strong position to initiate a reform of the Celtic usages. The essential beliefs and doctrines of the Celtic Church were the same as those held in Western Europe, but owing to its remote situation, cut off for centuries by the strife of the Dark Ages, the Celtic organisation and liturgy were based on old-fashioned customs. So, though out of touch, the Celtic Church, or, perhaps better, the Scottish Church, was in no sense an independent body, for then, as in the present day, there were considerable differences of observation among those who acknowledged the Pope and were accepted by him. There are today churches within the scope of Rome whose liturgies are unlike the Roman; some may even be celebrated in languages other than Latin by married clergy. Thus, the Scottish Church of Queen Margaret's day differed less in some ways from the Roman usage than several which are under the present Papal rule. Though Queen Margaret used her influence to bring the Church more up to date, it was left to her sons, David I in particular, to revolutionise the whole ecclesiastical structure and civil administration of the country.

The loosely organised church was reconstructed and divided into dioceses, each with its bishop and cathedral church, while various orders of monks and canons superseded the Celtic clergy. The latter were given the option to join the new communities, which is significant, for had there been more than mere custom at stake this certainly would not have happened. The Benedictines of Canterbury sent monks to Dunfermline, others from Reading went to the Isle of May, while white Cistercians came from Rievaulx to Melrose and Augustinian canons from St-Quentin, near Beauvais, to Jedburgh. Another innovation was the granting of tracts of land to settlers from England or further afield, who, in return, were expected to keep law and order and to provide the king with men in time of war. One of the first things these people did after obtaining their lands was to build a strong castle of timber, often upon the top of an artificial mound of earth known as a mote. Near this castle they erected a church for their own use and for that of their retainers and dependents on the barony. One of the earliest of these grants to be recorded was that of Ednam in Berwickshire by King Edgar, David's elder brother, about 1105 to Thor Longus, who there built and endowed a church.

With the contemporary founding of episcopal dioceses it was natural that the new churches should come under the spiritual direction of the bishop in whose territory they stood, and that the baronial areas they served should thus become ecclesiastical subdivisions. Hence the parish normally corresponded with the barony. Since then the boundaries may well have altered. Should a large barony be divided, another church and parish might be founded, or the lands of a great lord might be so wide that they contained several parishes. Later, when parts of the country became more populous, new parishes were formed, or when people were thin on the ground and the endowments could not support two churches there were sometimes unions. By and large, however, especially in rural districts, the broad outline remains, and even when the present parish church is a modern building it may stand on the site which was selected in the 12th century. In such case a mound or some other trace of the castle where the founder baron dwelt can often be found near it. The Bass of Inverurie is such a mote or castle hill and, though the church was removed from beside it in 1774, the kirk-yard still remains.

Many of the families to whom the sons of Margaret, or their successors Malcolm IV (1153–65) and William the Lion (1165–1214), granted land were foreigners such as de Vaux, de Avenel, de Sulis, Freskyne the Fleming and so on. It was natural that these men should have their churches built in a manner which was familiar to them and according to the style prevalent in Western Europe. Further, some of the craftsmen came from the south. For instance, Dunfermline Abbey, founded in 1128, has details reminiscent of Durham Cathedral which was being built at the time. From the evidence of their marks it appears that masons went from Dunfermline to Dalmeny Kirk in West Lothian around 1150. Subsequent marks at Dalmeny correspond to some of those at Leuchars in Fife, which is of slightly later date, and thus the contemporary style and mode of building was carried round the country. This style, in which the barons, and indeed everyone else in north-west Europe, built in the 12th century is called Romanesque, or in England, Norman. Its origins were in the classical

DUNNING, PERTHSHIRE

A tall Romanesque tower

DESKFORD, BANFFSHIRE

The sacrament house, the medieval emphasis

NEWBURN, FIFE

The pulpit, the reformed emphasis

PITCAIRN, PERTHSHIRE

The typical country church for five hundred years

buildings of ancient Rome, adapted for the Christianised
basilica and modified through France to Normandy,
from there it came to England with the Conquest,
though the English genius made the English version
unmistakably English. Thus in its English or Norman
form it appeared in Scotland. In those days the Border
was fluid and there was much coming and going, for
David I, among others, held lands and titles in England,
so there was no appreciable difference in style between
the English and the Scottish churches of the period.

The actual shape or plan of a church, like other
buildings, is derived from the use to which it is put,
and the essentials of these 12th-century churches were
twofold. In the first place they had to shelter an altar,
for the church was built for the altar and not the altar
for the church. Secondly they had to accommodate the
people assisting at the service. These two basic requirements are clearly seen in the Romanesque churches of
this country. The section containing the altar is known
as the chancel. This word is derived from the *cancellos*
or screen and implies that the sanctuary was screened off
from the people's space or nave. Nave is derived from
the Latin *navis*, a ship.

The Romanesque chancel tended to be nearly square
on plan, for apart from the altar few other furnishings
were necessary. It was lit by very small, round-headed
windows, for since glass was not in general use these
narrow windows were filled with cloth, thin horn or
wooden shutters which were only opened at time of
service. Often there was a window in the east wall above
the altar, one on the south wall and occasionally one on
the north wall. Examples of these little chancels may

B 5

be seen at Birnie in Moray, Legerwood in Berwickshire, Cruggleton in Wigtownshire, Aberdour in Fife and Duddingston in Edinburgh. None of them, however, look in the least as they did in the 12th century. In some the windows have been enlarged, in all cases the wooden roofs have been replaced and the wall surfaces stripped to the stone, instead of being thinly coated with lime wash or plaster and painted.

The supreme importance of the altar standing in this chancel or sanctuary cannot be over-estimated, for it was to the altar that Christ came in the flesh. There was no question of symbolism in this matter, for this was a tenet of faith, believed in as a fact. When consecrated, the bread and wine became literally the Body and Blood of the Saviour. This belief, in the light of what was to happen later, is of profound importance and must always be borne in mind when considering the architecture of a medieval church. The people might not understand a word of the liturgy, they might not often partake of Communion, but they did believe that at the consecration Christ was in their midst both in the spirit and in substance.

No altars of the 12th century survive, but from examples in other countries we know that they were made of stone, short in length and rather deep back to front. They were very simply furnished. The essential ornament was a cover, for the consecrated altar represented Christ, and only on Good Friday was this removed. On the mensa, as the top slab is called, one or two candlesticks might be placed to enable the priest to read the liturgy, but these would be removed at the end of a service. Altar crucifixes were known at the time, but it is unlikely that small rural churches had such valuable possessions. Processional crosses were sometimes set up behind the altar on the entry of the ministers, but often this ornament was lacking, for not until after our Reformation, hundreds of years later, was a crucifix obligatory on the Roman altar.

In some of the grander Romanesque churches the altar was placed in a semicircular extension, known as an apse, which projected eastwards from the chancel. The apse was derived from the Roman basilica and was extensively used on the Continent but rather less in Scotland and England. Some have suggested that this omission was because the earlier churches in Britain did not have this feature, but a more likely explanation is greater cost of building on the curve and the provision of an extra archway opening from the chancel into the apse. Thus, much as the founders might have liked to build an apse, expense prevented it for all but the wealthy. We find the powerful Gospatrick built an apse at Dalmeny and so did Robert de Quincey at Leuchars. Another church of similar plan, but larger, is Tyningham which, alas, is very fragmentary; only the foundations and the arches of the chancel and apse remain. These churches are throughout richer than was normal. At Bunkle in Berwickshire a simple little apse is the sole remaining portion of the building. There is another at Borthwick in Midlothian, but to all intents and purposes it has been rebuilt.

The nave, or people's part of the church, was invariably larger than the chancel. It was usually a little wider and instead of being roughly square it might be anything from one and a half to two times as long as broad.

There was no seating in the nave so it was sparsely furnished. The people either stood or knelt on the floor; a practice which has by no means died out in some parts of Christendom. It was divided from the chancel by a round-headed arch whose mouldings were sometimes very elaborate. Many such arches remain: grand ones at Dalmeny, Leuchars and Duddingston, and simpler examples at Legerwood, Birnie, Peterhead and Monymusk. Though there are few traces, there would be a great cross or rood above this arch, either supported by the screen which filled the arch or on a beam above that. There would be a small altar on either side of the arch and the remains of these may be seen at Tyningham. Near the door was the only other major furnishing, namely the font. Most medieval fonts remaining in Scotland are so simple that it is difficult to date them. None have been in constant use till the present day, but a few have found their way back into the kirk. Being large stone bowls they were found useful for various purposes after the Reformation; many have been adapted as drinking troughs for cattle, some as garden ornaments, while others have been dug up from underneath church floors. There are fonts which may date from the 12th century restored to use at Linton and Birnie.

The main entrance to the parish church was, according to the examples left to us, towards the west end of the south wall of the nave. This doorway was as elaborate as possible and at Dalmeny it is intricately carved with a variety of subjects and surmounted by an interlacing arcade. Other good examples may be found at Chirnside, Stobo and Uphall. Unfortunately, as will be seen later, the position of such doorways did not suit the internal planning of Reformed worship, and many are now blocked up or even partly built over by later additions. Such is the state of things at Abercorn, Ratho, Duddingston and Kirkliston, the latter a late example but very grand. Often there was a north doorway on the opposite wall of the nave but this was never so elaborate. Indeed at Uphall it is reduced to the simplest possible square-headed opening (now partially built up to form a window). Some of the north doorways are also blocked up, such as those of Dunning and Lamington, a particularly fine example, while at Kirkliston, though preserved, the north doorway has been rebuilt twice since 1822 owing to additions.

In many places the west gable of the nave was the termination of the building, but in some of the richer churches a tower was erected at this end. Several of these towers survive and are of considerable interest, being tall and narrow and in general shape, though not in detail, akin to Saxon work in England. Fine examples may be seen at Dunning, Markinch and Muthill, also at Kirkliston though here the tower is later (probably after 1200) and reduced in height. Dalmeny retains an arch leading into the tower space, but the squat tower is modern. Uphall also retains its tower arch and parts of the original walling, but the tower itself has been reduced in height and much altered. These towers were built to hold bells and when they retain their full height there are always openings near the top to emit their sound. They may also have been used in time of trouble as a place of refuge, for certainly in those days they were the strongest building in the parish.

Such, very briefly, was the Romanesque parish church in Scotland. All those which remain are small country kirks, though some of them, such as Dalmeny and Leuchars, are notable examples. Bigger ones are known to have existed in the burghs, but the town churches were all so much rebuilt in the 15th and 16th centuries that the Romanesque work has largely vanished. In the 12th century they were brighter places than they are now, for the exteriors were whitewashed. The effect of this can still be seen in Denmark where the tradition remains, and small Romanesque churches rising white above the green fields are noteworthy features of the landscape. The interiors were also lighter with brightly coloured frescoes on the white plaster depicting scenes from the Bible stories. But none of this remains for us to see.

CHAPTER II

# FIRST POINTED: THE POOR RELATION

At the beginning of the 13th century Scotland was a reasonably peaceful country, friendly with England and other states. Many of the great monasteries had already been founded, but the Cistercian order, though the strictest, were still erecting new houses throughout the country such as Glenluce (1192), Culross (1217), Deer (1219), Balmerino (1227) and finally, the last of their great abbeys, Sweetheart (1275). There were also three priories of the Valliscaulians, a new order from France; Pluscarden founded by the king, Alexander II, Ardchattan and Beauly, all dating from 1230. The cathedrals were being rebuilt at Elgin, Glasgow, Dornoch, Dunblane and other places. There was in fact a wonderful flowering of architecture, for Gothic with its pointed arches and soaring vaults was arising throughout Christendom. From France, the birthplace of the style, to the Holy Sepulchre at Jerusalem, superbly beautiful churches were being built: in England, Lincoln and Salisbury; in France, Chartres and later the amazing engineering feat of the choir of Beauvais. In Spain at Toledo and León, far in the north at Trondheim in Norway and yet further away, eastward, at Nicosia in Cyprus, great Gothic churches were arising and the Christian world was united from north to south and east to west by a magnificent common architecture.

11

Scotland shared in this glory of the 13th century, for all the cathedral and abbey churches already mentioned were examples of this new genius. However, such churches were planned and built for purposes which now have no place in the Church of Scotland, and such as are still in use do not make ideal parish churches in spite of the beauty of their architecture. Unfortunately the average parish church of the 13th century in Scotland was not impressive in spite of, or rather because of, the monastic splendour.

In order to understand the general meanness of the medieval parish church in Scotland it is necessary to explain what became of their emoluments. As already related, the feudal barons founded churches on their estates. These churches were endowed with a plough-gate of land (about 120 acres) and the teinds. These teinds amounted to a tenth of the annual produce of the parish and under ideal conditions they were gathered by the rector, or ruler. They were then allocated for various purposes, part for the rector as his stipend, part for the maintenance of the church and its services, part for the poor of the parish and, in some cases, part for the upkeep of the bishop or the cathedral. Had matters been allowed to remain like that the pastoral ministry in the parishes might have been very different to what it became, the parish churches would have been finer and larger and, no doubt, the poor would have fared better. However, it was to turn out otherwise, for many of the founders or their descendants bequeathed their churches to some monastery. This meant that the abbot or prior was the nominal rector and that the teinds were collected on behalf of his monastery. The religious houses were not particularly interested in parishes, other than their produce, so in order to minister to the needs of the people they paid a pittance to a secular priest or even a deacon to act as vicar, from the Latin *vicarius*, a deputy. No doubt these vicars did what they could for their church and parish, but, unless some generous donor appeared, lack of means prevented their doing much. That a large proportion of the churches in the country belonged to the monasteries may be realised by the fact that the abbeys of Dunfermline, Arbroath, Holyrood and Kelso each owned the teinds of more than thirty parishes. These parishes were not necessarily near the monastery, and when David, Earl of Garioch and of Huntingdon, brother of Kings Malcolm IV and William the Lion, founded the Abbey of Lindores in Fife in 1199 he endowed it with nine parishes in Aberdeenshire and two in England. Others were even further afield, for Scone Abbey held Kildonan in Sutherland and Holyrood was interested in Rodel in Harris.

The religious houses were not the only drain on the parish system; there were other institutions to keep up, namely the cathedrals and, later, the collegiate churches. The ruling body of the cathedral church was called a Chapter and was presided over by a Dean. In the normal way each member of a cathedral chapter was also rector of a parish and hence drew its revenue. These prebendaries, or canons, may have spent some time in their parish but records rather confirm that they did not. In any event many of these ecclesiastics were pluralists, holding several such livings in various parts of the country, so obviously they could not do a good job at them all. Accordingly they too appointed a vicar in the parish and another at the cathedral, known as a vicar choral, to represent them at the daily choir services. The canon was then free to do what he liked on a very fair income, but the parishes suffered. Chapters varied in size but Glasgow had no fewer than thirty-two canons. This meant thirty-one livings (one being a temporal barony) for their use out of nearly two hundred parishes in that diocese. In the smaller dioceses the proportion was of course much greater, as at Brechin where, with under thirty parishes, there were fourteen canons.

This may seem a somewhat complicated tale and at first sight to have little to do with the actual building of parish churches, but in fact it has quite a lot to do with it for, remember, part of the teinds, under ideal conditions, went to support the church and its services. In Scotland, perhaps more than any country in Europe, these teinds were appropriated for purposes outwith the parish. Hence though we may have the ruins of many fine abbeys which became useless at the Reformation, we possess remarkably few fine medieval parish churches. The endowments of the parishes helped to sustain the monasteries, and little was left for the country kirk. As will be seen later, the town church was another matter and many of the larger ones are still in being. The country church was seldom large. It is unprofitable to mourn their loss as they were generally quite inadequate for an increasing population, and so were rebuilt bigger and perhaps better at some time after the Reformation.

No doubt a certain lack of First Pointed architecture in the parishes is partly due to the fact that the Romanesque churches were still comparatively new and still adequate with regard to size. One thing, however, which was becoming cramped owing to the more elaborate services based on the Salisbury or Sarum Use was the square sanctuary of the previous century. In several places this was enlarged, as at Uphall where it was lengthened eastward to about double its previous size. The addition is noticeable owing to its thinner walls and narrow pointed lancet windows. The same thing happened at Gullane in East Lothian, Stobo in Peeblesshire and St. Blane's in Bute.

It was during the 13th century that, externally at any rate, the whole building tended to become a unit. That is, there was seldom a gable and stone arch between the nave and chancel, and this is important, for it was destined to become the normal plan of the smaller church till long after the Reformation. Internally, of course, there was a screen between the sanctuary and the nave dividing the interior into roughly a third part for the chancel and two-thirds for the nave.

Although roofless, one of the best preserved churches of this period is Abdie in Fife. It was in use till the present church was built in 1827 so there have naturally been alterations. Nevertheless the long narrow plan is clear with its pointed windows and stout buttresses.

Another church, smaller and somewhat earlier in date, is Auchindoir in Aberdeenshire. It also is roofless and, as it was in use till another church was built in 1811, it too has later features both medieval and post-Reformation. Its plan is also a rectangle with a south doorway, dating from shortly after 1200, still in excellent preservation and finely ornamented.

Prestonkirk in East Lothian retains the east end of its 13th-century chancel—long since appropriated as the burial aisle of the Buchan Hepburns of Smeaton Hepburn. This is rather a more elaborate example than most with its three long eastern lancets divided by elegant buttresses.

In the north at Mortlach, in Banffshire, is a simple church of this period, one of the few still in use. The east end contains a couple of narrow lancet windows with a third high above in the gable and there is a round-headed north doorway. The plan, ignoring later additions, is a plain rectangle with thick walls, and the fact of its being larger than usual has probably led to its preservation. Still further north at Kilchrist in Ross is a complete and little altered church of this type; roofed but not in use. Other small examples in ruins may be seen at Pert and Logie in Angus and Cowie in Kincardineshire.

There is no doubt that the basic plan of the small Scottish parish church for the next six hundred years was laid in the 13th century, and as it was so simple it is very hard to date some of them accurately unless there are definite features which have been untouched throughout the centuries. As indicated this plan is a rectangle with low walls and one roof running from the east to the west gable. This was quite the most economical way to build a church. They were narrow, seldom more than twenty feet wide inside, often considerably less, so there was no great difficulty in finding the roof timbers. The length varied, presumably according to the size of the parish, and might be anything from nearly a hundred feet, like Abdie, down to just over fifty, like Auchindoir. The architectural treatment was equally simple, there might be buttresses at the corners, set at right angles at this period, or perhaps diagonally if later in date. The windows were narrow lancets, but since these persisted till the Reformation it cannot always be assumed that they are 13th-century work. The east gable normally contains two or three in a row, while others are set along the south wall. There are seldom any on the north wall, for until 1800 it was very common in Scotland to have no windows on the cold side. The doorways were generally simply moulded, sometimes round-headed rather than pointed. The main doorway, as in the previous century, was on the south wall and near the west end thereof. In some places there was a north doorway opposite and occasionally a small doorway on the south side of the chancel for the use of the priest. Vestries were not usual at this period, for the priest vested at the altar. The vestments in most cases were kept in a wooden chest near the altar at which they were worn.

Inside, these churches were equally simple. The nave would be without seats, with the font at the west end near the door. Towards the east was a wooden screen with a doorway in the middle. On either side of this doorway was a small altar, while above was the great crucifix or rood. Within the screen was the high altar against the east wall. The walls themselves would be plastered and in some cases painted with scenes from the life of Our Lord or of the saints. In England and other countries it was common to have St. Christopher, the patron saint of travellers, depicted on the north wall opposite the main doorway and it is likely that the same obtained in Scotland.

Though this was the most simple and the most general

type of parish church there were others more elaborate with clearly defined chancels such as may be seen at the ruined church of Buittle in Kirkcudbrightshire.

In the towns they were still more developed with side aisles divided from the nave by arcades. At Lanark, for instance, are the remains of an unusual church which had a double nave divided by a row of arches which still stand. This building was used till 1777 when the present church was erected. Most of the town churches were rebuilt at a later date, and so the more developed architecture of this period can best be studied in the cathedral and monastic churches.

## CHAPTER III

## SCOTS GOTHIC: THE RICH BURGHERS

WHEN in 1286 Alexander III rode over a cliff near Kinghorn to his death, a prosperous epoch in Scottish history was closed and the country was plunged into the miseries of the War of Independence, which may be said to have lasted a hundred years. Wars, as we know today, are not propitious times for church building; in fact the reverse, for then, as now, churches were desecrated or burnt without scruple. Hence not only are there few remains of parish churches dating from the earlier part of the 14th century, but the foundation of new monasteries and friar's houses all but stopped. Churchmen, led by their bishops, were perhaps the most patriotic section of the community and so had matters other than building to think about. That the oaks obtained to erect the cathedral spire at Glasgow were turned into siege engines by Bishop Wishart need occasion no surprise.

When the situation became quieter towards the end of the century, we find that churches were again planned but they were rather different to those which had gone before; except of course for the small rural church, still a long narrow rectangle. One of the main reasons for a change in style was, naturally enough, that Scotland was heartily sick of England and Englishmen; the close connection of the 12th and 13th centuries had been broken. So Scotland glanced at France for architectural inspiration and then got on with things in her own way. With the revival of the wasted country an increase of trade with the Continent encouraged the towns to expand, and the merchants, whose wealth was not dependent on the land, to assume a greater role. Their travels awakened them to influences furth of Scotland, and it is largely to them we owe the large burgh kirks rebuilt during the 15th century. Many kirks had suffered during the war and doubtless others were becoming too small for their congregations. Nor was this all: with a more general increase in wealth there was an important religious urge towards enlarging churches by the addition of chantry chapels.

The Roman Church teaches that there is a state called Purgatory to which souls go after death and are prepared for the joys of Heaven. Moreover, through the intercession of the saints, it is thought possible for those on earth to help the departed in Purgatory. It was natural therefore that those who could afford to do so founded an altar in the parish church and endowed a chaplain who could say Mass for their deceased relatives, for themselves and for their family when the time came. St. Giles', then the only parish church in Edinburgh, owes its wide plan to the addition of such chapels built and endowed both by private individuals and by trade guilds. This church was probably founded early in the 12th century and a Romanesque north doorway existed till towards the end of the 18th century. The fabric of the church was damaged several times during the War of Independence, most seriously by the English under Richard II in 1385. The citizens quickly set about

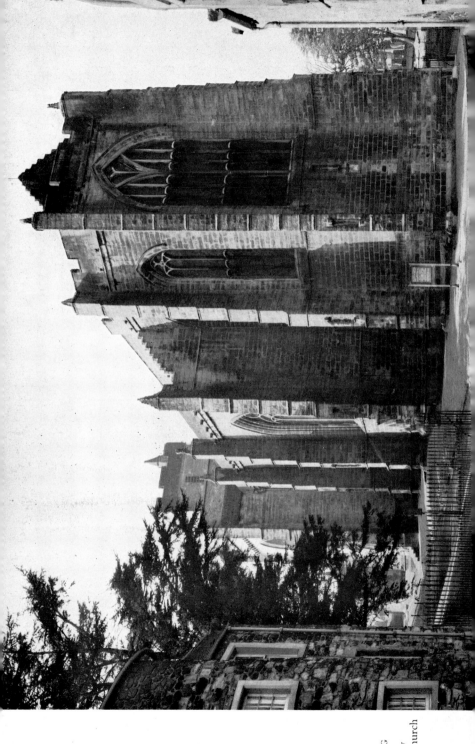

STIRLING

A stately
burgh church

DOUGLAS, LANARKSHIRE

The 15th-century tomb of James, 7th Earl of Douglas

repairs and added a series of five chapels beyond the south aisle of the nave, which, according to the contract, were to follow the design of a chapel at Holyrood. Soon after two chapels (known as the Albany Aisle) were added to the north of the nave and then two more on the same side, but further east. About 1460 the chancel was lengthened a bay, and the choir vault heightened. Around the same time, the Preston Aisle of three bays was added to the south, and in the early 16th century the Holy Blood and St. John's Chapels were built still further southward.

Though the church was much enlarged by all this building, there can have been little alteration to what we should now call the seating space. Each chapel was small in itself and was screened from its neighbours. Any morning the visitor to the medieval St. Giles' might have found Mass being celebrated at several altars and at each a few people standing around, some no doubt drawn by the alms which were sometimes distributed on these occasions. It is hard for us today to understand that a church like St. Giles' was built for purposes so totally different from the one it now serves and that, as a result, its interior appearance would be utterly strange. The choir was surrounded by screens and fitted with stalls for the vicar and chaplains (later Provost and Canons, for it became Collegiate in 1466), who there sang the daily offices, services the public were not necessarily expected to attend. At the west end of the choir would be the rood screen with its loft and great crucifix. The central space of the nave would be open and in it would stand the pulpit against one of the pillars, possibly about half-way down so that people could gather round in a semicircle (the same arrangement, as we shall see, which the Reformers adopted). There would, by our standards, be a small organ on the rood loft or floor of the choir, and the aisles would be filled with altars surrounded by painted wooden screens. The walls and vaults were plastered and brightly coloured. Yet in spite of its present 19th-century arrangements there is much of interest to study in St. Giles'; notably the fine 15th-century vaulting of the choir and the Scottish type of piers in the aisles. The outside of the church was entirely refaced in a most unimaginative manner in 1829, and only the grand crowned steeple, dating from about 1500, was happily left alone.

St. Giles', Edinburgh, was not the largest parish church in Scotland, for that honour belonged to St. Nicholas, Aberdeen, a church which has suffered even more from rebuilding than St. Giles' has from refacing. The medieval nave has vanished, for it was rebuilt, somewhat shorter, in 1755, but the ancient transepts remain, though altered, together with the tower arches dating from about 1200. The tower and spire themselves were burnt in 1874 and replaced in a pretentious manner entirely unlike the original. The 15th-century choir with its eastern apse was demolished in 1836, when the present Gothic structure designed by Archibald Simpson took its place. However, as the ground slopes sharply eastward, a small crypt was formed under that end of the choir, and this is comparatively untouched. It is a most interesting structure dating from 1420–35 and contains a good collection of 16th- and 17th-century woodwork.

Another very large church was that of Dundee.

Today, alas, nothing whatever remains of the medieval structure except the imposing western tower which, rising to a height of 165 feet, is by far the grandest thing of its type in the country. From evidence of the fabric it was intended to finish it with a crown like the parish church of Edinburgh, but this was never achieved. Most of this tower dates from the mid-15th century.

Further up the Tay, in Perth, is St. John's which, like St. Giles', Edinburgh, was entirely refaced outside though the lead spire is the oldest in the country. It is a cruciform structure of about the same internal length as St. Giles', but does not have the numerous chapels added on either side. There is no vaulting except for the north porch and the crossing under the tower which has holes in the ribs for bell ropes. From the evidence of an inscription on the south-east pier the elegant choir arcades were built about 1440, but the low and rather dark nave is undoubtedly later, and is in any case much rebuilt. The south-west pier of the tower contains a spiral stair and the doorway giving access from it to the rood loft remains, together with some of the corbels which supported the loft. In this church hangs one of the two medieval chandeliers remaining in Scotland— the other is in Brechin Cathedral.

Still another church of similar scale, which was being built about the same time, is the Holy Rood at Stirling. Like Dundee this church has a western, not a central tower, and, like Aberdeen, an eastern apse for the high altar. As with the others it was the effort of several generations, for the nave dates from 1414 and the apse was not completed till 1520. Both choir and nave have vaulted aisles and the latter retains its original timber roof over the central space. From the nave there originally opened three chantry chapels but only one, St. Andrew's, on the north side, remains—a small and attractive vaulted building. The nave at Stirling has round piers which vaguely follow earlier precedents as do the contemporary pillars at Dunkeld Cathedral. As the ground falls to the east, the apse with its towering buttresses is a most impressive composition. Unfortunately parts of the old fabric were altered during a renovation shortly before the last war.

Less than twenty miles east is another great parish church—St. Michael's, Linlithgow. This church is less altered and is also more homogeneous than any of those so far mentioned. It consists of a western tower, formerly capped by a crown of four flying buttresses, an aisled nave and choir under one continuous roof, an eastern apse and transeptal chapels to north and south. A church has long stood on the site, but the present structure was largely rebuilt about the middle of the 15th century and not finished till the 1530's. Standing, as it does, next to the Royal Palace, the kings, particularly James IV and James V, took considerable interest in its construction and several of their contributions are recorded. Like other large kirks Linlithgow had its quota of chantry altars, and records of their dedications together with many of the bequests to their chaplains for singing Masses for the dead are preserved. Though from the Reformation till 1896 only part of this church was in use, the Town Council fortunately maintained the whole fabric.

The third big parish church of the Lothians, St. Mary's, Haddington, must have been the most impressive

with its crowned central tower, well-developed transepts
and vaulted choir. Alas, the inhabitants of Haddington
did not maintain it all after the Reformation as did
the burghers of Linlithgow, nor were they sufficiently
numerous to warrant their dividing it into several
churches as at Edinburgh. So today the choir and transepts are in ruin and there is no longer a crown on the
roofless tower. The nave only is used and it has been
altered to make it convenient for galleries. It is indeed
fortunate that so much survived, for the English ordered
its demolition in 1548, and though they did not achieve
their purpose, some damage was done. The structure
is largely 15th century, and, like other town kirks, the
interior was enriched by chantry chapels which occupied
the aisles and transepts. Much of the detail is character-
istically Scottish, such as the double western doorway
under a well-wrought round-headed arch, the pillars
and the blank east walls to the aisles and transepts. This
last feature, which may also be seen in Linlithgow and
Stirling, was probably contrived as a background for
towering reredoses imported from Flanders or Lübeck.

In 1412 and 1415 new churches were begun at St.
Andrews and Cupar respectively. From the evidence
which can be obtained, these churches were very similar
and, being only a few miles apart, it is probable that they
were designed by the same person. Both were aisled
rectangles with a tower at the north-west corner. At
both the tower remains, but very little else. After many
alterations St. Andrews was rebuilt in 1908 on old lines.
At Cupar a new church was erected in 1785 on the
eastern part of the old building and only the arches of
the north aisle between it and the tower were suffered

to remain. The St. Andrews rebuild, though meritorious in detail and hardly medieval in arrangement, does give a broad idea of the scale and size of a town kirk at the beginning of the 15th century.

Two other burghs in Fife had large medieval churches, namely Dysart, now a ruin, and Crail, which latterly became collegiate. The tower at Dysart, the only considerable portion remaining, is a fine structure and terminates with parapet and cap-house similar to a contemporary castle. Crail, no mean kirk, has also a grand steeple, charming early 19th-century pews and much 17th-century woodwork, though the latter cannot be seen to advantage.

By the 15th century the influence of the monastic houses was on the wane. Endowments were less generous than previously, and religious fervour was not what it had been. The office of Abbot and Prior came to be looked on as a sinecure for the younger sons of the nobility whether they had priestly vocation or not. Perhaps even more significant, the wealthy were no longer so enthusiastic about burial in the choirs of their great churches where the monks could sing Masses for the repose of their souls. This did not mean that the nobles were any less anxious about the repose of their souls, but they did not appear to trust the monks to fulfil their obligations so well as they had of old. We have seen that the greater town churches were filled with altars founded by merchants and guilds for this purpose and that each had its chaplain. So it was that wealthy barons founded another type of establishment, often very directly under their own control, which a monastery could not be, in order to ensure that the utmost was done 'in perpetuity' for the departed. These establishments were called collegiate churches. They sometimes had nothing to do with parishes, but they are mentioned here because many were grafted on to an existing parish church and also because their building produced a distinctive Scottish ecclesiastical style of architecture. The organisation of a collegiate kirk was similar to that of a cathedral chapter in miniature. At its head was an official known as a Provost, a title still used in the Scottish Episcopal Church cathedrals, in those of Scandinavia and in the more recently created English foundations. Under the Provost were the number of prebendaries specified in the foundation charter, perhaps a couple of singing boys, and, in some cases, a few old pensioners or bedesmen. These people were supported by various endowments given by the founder which occasionally included the teinds of some parish which had not yet been appropriated by the monasteries or cathedrals. Needless to say, these establishments were encouraged by the Church, for they could set an example which might combat the disturbing teachings then filtering in from the Continent. Further, when they were connected with a parish church, one of the prebendaries was appointed to minister to the people; a possible improvement on a poor vicar. But, as the main function of the dignitaries of these churches was to sing the Divine Office daily and to say Masses for the souls of the founder and his family, it was the choir which received the first and most lavish attention. In fact, when there was no parish attached, the building was often not carried further than the choir, or perhaps the transepts. Roslin, for instance, never a parish church, was founded in 1447, over a hundred years before the Reformation, but the building was not carried beyond the choir though there are the beginnings of the east walls of the transepts. At Crichton and Seton (founded in 1449 and 1493 respectively) are fine vaulted, cruciform kirks where a nave has never been built. Other collegiate kirks were erected in connection with the Universities. The University of St. Andrews was founded in 1412 and later, within it, the colleges of St. Salvator, St. Leonard and St. Mary. The college kirk at the first was a completely new structure founded in 1450 by Bishop Kennedy and preaching to the people was one of its functions so, unlike the college chapels of Oxford or Cambridge, its main doorway opens to the street, not to the college court. St. Leonard's College was founded in 1512 and its chapel was an extension of the small parish kirk used by the layfolk within the Cathedral Priory precinct. It is interesting that, although the cathedral was the largest in Scotland, the people around it had a parish kirk of their own. Another University college kirk is that of King's, Aberdeen, commenced in 1500. Though it was built for a student body its main doorway also faces the street. Within is the only complete set of medieval college choir stalls in Britain.

These are all special cases with no particular reference to an ordinary parish, but one of the earliest collegiate kirks to be founded did have this association. That was Bothwell which Archibald, Earl of Douglas, endowed in 1397. Apparently he pulled down the chancel which then stood, left the parishioners with the Romanesque nave (rebuilt in 1833) and erected the splendid choir,

which remains to this day, for his provost and prebendaries, or canons, to sing their daily offices, shut off
by a screen from any disturbances in the nave. The
Bothwell choir is a fascinating building, for it is constructed entirely of stone. Within is a high-pointed
barrel vault supporting a steeply pitched roof of stone
slabs. This strong impressive style, rather heavy in
effect, is typical of the 15th century. Examples may be
seen at the collegiate churches of Dunglass (a ruin),
Corstorphine (now a parish kirk), Seton (in the custody
of the Ministry of Works), Crichton and, at its most
elaborate, Roslin.

Not all collegiate kirks were designed in this fireproof
construction and there are just as many which carry on
the tradition of timber roofs. Among those connected
with parishes may be mentioned Foulis Easter near
Dundee which was founded, as a college, by Lord Gray
in 1538. It is one of our most interesting mid-16th-
century churches of the simpler type, for though it has
the usual long rectangular plan the site of the choir
screen and loft is clearly defined, and further, some of
the painted woodwork of that screen still remains in the
church.

Two very late collegiate establishments were Cullen
in Banffshire, founded by Alexander Ogilvy of Deskford in 1543, and Biggar in Lanarkshire, founded by
Lord Fleming in 1545. Cullen is a charming composite
structure with a tremendous founder's tomb on the
north wall of the choir, and the splendid 17th-century
Seafield loft hanging from the south wall. The chapel
of St. Anne is covered with interesting carved inscrip-
tions and the whole effect is pleasantly informal, though

recently much marred by the removal of the external harling.

Biggar, though it has no elaborate founder's tomb, is more pretentious and is notable as one of the last churches to be built before the Reformation. It is cruciform with a low central tower. The nave, much rebuilt, may have been part of the previous parish kirk, and continued as such, but the choir and transepts are obviously the results of Lord Fleming's foundation. The former ends in a three-sided apse typical of the continental influence prevailing in Scotland at the time. Unfortunately all the wooden ceilings are of poor Victorian work, the walls are skinned of their plaster and the floor is so cluttered up with seats that it is hard to gain any idea of its medieval appearance from within.

In several cases these collegiate-cum-parish kirks have been entirely rebuilt except for a single aisle, containing the tombs of the founder's family, which has been retained as the burial place of their descendants. They are generally securely fastened up and in some cases the key is apparently lost. Nevertheless, there are often fine tombs within and the small fragments at Carnwath, Kilmaurs, Methven, Glamis and Guthrie are well worth a visit.

It is obviously impossible to enumerate all the later medieval work, but kirks were being built up till a few years before the Reformation in 1560. Many were doubtless of the long narrow plan and have been subsequently rebuilt, but when a church of some size was erected it may well remain. Two examples may be quoted; Whitekirk in East Lothian and Mid Calder in Midlothian. The former was much frequented by pilgrims in the middle ages, and the mid-15th-century kirk is a spacious cruciform structure with a central tower and elaborate south porch. The choir has a high-pointed barrel vault, typical of the period. Mid Calder, one of the latest and a most ambitious effort, was begun about 1540 by Peter Sandilands, the rector, a relative of the laird of Calder whose descendant, Lord Torphichen, still lives beside it. As with so many late medieval kirks, the work at Mid Calder did not advance beyond the choir, but in this case the contract for the whole job is preserved and so it is possible to envisage what was intended. As with the 14th-century chapels at St. Giles', Edinburgh, a model to be followed is quoted, namely St. Anthony's Chapel at St. Giles'. The medieval choir at Mid Calder is much finer than the average rural parish church, no doubt owing to the rector's family connection. Outside it is built of wrought ashlar, has large windows with simple tracery and a three-sided apse at the east end. Within it was to have been stone vaulted, but though this was never carried out the 19th-century plaster vaulting gives a fair idea of the intention.

When describing the Romanesque church it was emphasised that Holy Communion or Mass was the central act of medieval worship, and that at the consecration it was believed that the bread and wine became the Body and Blood of Christ. All the churches so far mentioned were built to this end, and, however humble they might be, the altar was a place apart, set aside for this most Holy Mystery—it could hardly be otherwise, given this belief. And further, the medieval church, not unnaturally, kept these Holy Elements within the sanctuary so that the priest could take them to the sick and dying for their spiritual comfort, and so that men might enter to pray in their presence. Whether we believe this or not it is quite impossible to understand why a medieval church was built in the way it was without at least trying to understand what it meant, for it was the central belief of Gothic Christendom. The reserved Sacrament, that is the Body of Christ retained in the church, dates from early Christian times. In the Romanesque and later churches there is left no trace in Scotland of how it was kept. There were various means employed and one of the most usual in England was a suspended pyx, which is a container, sometimes in the form of a dove, hanging above the high altar. In some parts of Scotland, the diocese of Aberdeen in particular, it became customary by the end of the 15th century to reserve the Sacrament in a small cupboard or aumbry in the wall on the north side of the high altar, a use common in Germany and other parts of the Continent at that time but little adopted in England.

This small cupboard was called a sacrament house as we know from a contemporary inscription in English at Deskford in Banffshire, and good examples may be seen at Cullen, Kinkell, Auchindoir, Kintore and Foulis Easter. A common motif in their decoration is that of two angels holding a monstrance. A monstrance is a vessel, generally of gold or silver gilt, in which the consecrated host or wafer was carried between two discs of glass for exposition to the people. Indeed at Auchindoir the whole outline of the sacrament house is that of a monstrance.

Of the altars on which the bread and wine were consecrated but little remains. They were too nearly associated with the Mass to be left alone and further, the space they occupied was later used for seating. They were simple stone structures, very functionally designed, unlike so much church furniture of today. The top slab, or mensa, had to be a single stone and on it five crosses were cut, one in the centre of the slab and one near each corner. On each of these crosses a small fire burnt during its consecration ceremony. Large slabs of this kind did not escape the attention of the Reformed tombstone makers and one, again set up in a place of honour, may be seen at King's College Chapel in Aberdeen with its crosses among later carving. There is a well-preserved mensa in the sacristy at Corstorphine and two were recently found buried in the ruined church at Blair Atholl. The simplicity of these altars is explained by the fact that they were never seen except on Good Friday, which was the only day in the year when they were unclothed. The uncovered table was entirely foreign to the medieval church except when the most tragic scenes of the Passion had to be forcibly impressed upon the people. Needless to say, nothing remains in any parish church of the coverings of their altars. Behind the altars were set up carved reredoses of stone or wood, brightly painted, which depicted scenes from the Life of Our Lord, the Virgin or the Saints. A few battered fragments remain; there are some broken stones at Linlithgow illustrating scenes from the Passion. Likewise there are no chalices or patens remaining from these days. No country in Europe has so little to show in this respect as Scotland. The essential vessels of the Communion certainly existed in considerable numbers as we know from inventories, but all have vanished.

The other Sacrament requiring a definite piece of furniture, namely Baptism, is represented rather better. There are a few fonts which have been preserved and some are once more set up in churches. In medieval days they stood near the door, the threshold of life in the Church to which the newborn infant was taken. One of the finest is at Inverkeithing, a 16th-century bowl surrounded by angels bearing heraldic shields. A simple 15th-century example was dug up in St. Mahew's Chapel near Cardross in 1954.

RADIO!

The church bell was another feature which influenced medieval life to a considerable extent, for in the days before watches and wireless its sound punctuated the day from early morning till evening. There are several dating from the 15th and 16th centuries in the towers and bellcotes of Scotland and at Stirling, Linlithgow, Uphall, Elgin and Foulis Easter they may still be heard, while in other places medieval bells are carefully preserved in the church as at Bo'ness and St. Giles', Edinburgh.

The departed were not only remembered in the Masses sung for their souls, but by many splendid tombs scattered throughout the country where the knight and his lady lie tranquilly beneath richly carved canopies, or the priest is commemorated either by his effigy or by a plain slab with his chalice and book cut upon it. The priests and lairds were generally laid to rest within the church, in the chancel or a chantry chapel, while the common folk were buried outside in the kirkyard which was dominated by a large stone cross southward of the church. That any kirkyard crosses should have survived the turmoil of later years is surprising, but there are two in Moray at Dallas and Duffus.

No picture of the medieval church can possibly be given in so short a sketch, nor is there any building left to us which gives the slightest idea of what a church looked like in those days. The numerous 'restorations' carried out all over the country during the last seventy or eighty years have done much in the way of preservation and maintenance, but not one of them has gone further, there has been no attempt to catch the brilliance of colour of the middle ages. Arrangements obviously have to be quite different, for the use is different, but uneven stone walls and 'natural' oak furnishings can never give the faintest idea of the ancient internal appearance of our kirks. Perhaps the best place to see a restoration showing the lines of medieval arrangement is the Church of the Greyfriars (now Sisters of Mercy) in Elgin, though this is a monastic not a parish conception.

The small chapel of St. Mahew near Cardross, also in Roman Catholic hands, is likewise restored on medieval lines as it is harled without and plastered within—a foil to a painted reredos, rood screen and statues.

As we have seen, the parish kirk was always inclined to fare badly from the financial point of view owing to abuses of various kinds, and in due course the whole system became so rotten that it fell suddenly, leaving the parish kirk as the sole kind of kirk with any significance. The cathedral, monastic, friary and collegiate kirks, all lost their status and their function, so the parish kirk came into its own in spiritual matters at the Reformation, though, as it happened, it was not to be much better off financially.

## CHAPTER IV

# THE SEVENTEENTH CENTURY:
## REFORMED PLANNING

THE official date of the Reformation is 1560, for in that year the Estates, by Acts, which incidentally did not receive Royal assent, set up John Knox's Calvanistic Church in place of the Roman Church. At that time, we are led to understand, the ecclesiastical buildings of the country were pulled down by infuriated mobs. A most wasteful beginning for a new regime! It is true that much damage was done, and perhaps in some cases more than was intended. There was an intention, and its purpose was to 'cleanse' the interiors of the churches of all furniture offensive to Calvanistic policy. Hence altars with their reredoses, statues, crucifixes and so on were cast out and burnt or broken up, but the instructions went on to say that windows, doors, and even non-structural objects were to be preserved. This injunction may not always have been heeded to the letter, but the fact remains that not many buildings were structurally damaged at the time, certainly very few parish kirks. Even at some of the monasteries the monks were allowed to stay on till they died—Dom Thomas Ross was signing deeds at Pluscarden twenty-six years later and the Abbot at Sweetheart was at his abbey till after 1600. The reforming party could gain nothing by pulling down the kirks they so badly needed for themselves.

LADYKIRK, BERWICKSHIRE

Typical Scottish work of about 1500. The tower is 18th century

BURNTISLAND, FIFE

A late 16th-century experiment. The tower is 18th century

This vindication of the early Reformers does not necessarily mean that the churches were in perfect condition. In the south most of them were far from it after Henry VIII's savage raids only some sixteen years before; his orders to burn and destroy were explicit enough, and it is unlikely, in view of the unsettled state of the country at the time, that much patching up had been done. The family and clan feuds, both Border and Highland, often left kirks in a poor way and last, but not least, that common complaint of our own time, 'lack of maintenance', was rife. Maintenance can never have been a strong point in small kirks for better reasons than obtain today. So on the eve of a great religious upheaval when many of the parishioners were careless in their obligations and many of the ecclesiastical superiors were entirely uninterested, being laymen merely drawing revenues, the kirks must have been in a sorry state.

In its early days the new Church was short of both ministers and money, so many of the parishes had to be united under one minister or even under a reader. Thus many churches fell to ruin, as those which were superfluous were abandoned. No one was interested in old kirks for their own sake, and a ruin always made a good quarry, so some of them vanished altogether.

So much for destruction and decay, but once the Reformers had obtained a kirk, how did they wish to arrange it? Visually the whole emphasis of the interior changed. The altar against the east wall which had previously been the essential feature of a church had vanished and now for the celebration of Holy Communion only a table was required. This table was set in the midst of the people, thus the chancel was not necessary. The minister needed a pulpit from which to expound the Word and the position of a pulpit is determined only by the place which is best and most central for people to see and hear.

Thus the pulpit was also among the people, as in fact it had often been, for the Roman Church was quite as practical in its arrangements as the Reformed. In our long, narrow kirks one or other of the ends was impracticable and so the pulpit came to be placed centrally on one of the side walls, generally the south, so that the preacher had the light behind him, and could better study the effect of his discourse upon the people.

That the pulpit was the important item of furniture is clear enough from the first Book of Discipline. It exhorts that the kirks be quickly repaired and arrangements made 'with such preparation within as appertaineth as well to the Majesty of the Word of God as unto the ease and commodity of the people'.

Further, the reader who conducted early morning prayers and the preliminaries of the main services before the minister entered, had to be provided for. He had to have his lectern or 'letteroun', as it was called. The pulpit stood in the most central place in the church, so obviously the next best place was just below and in front of it. Thus here it was placed.

The people built their own pews or lofts in various places, all facing inwards to the pulpit. If there was a structural chancel arch, part of the chancel might be utilised by the local laird for his loft and the remainder became his burial place if it were not that already.

On the other hand, if the nave was big enough to

hold everybody the chancel was often walled off and left to ruin. At Kirkliston and Dunning, for instance, there is nothing left of it whatever, at Dalkeith most of it is a sorry ruin, while at Legerwood, Monymusk and other places the chancel has been rescued and re-roofed within comparatively recent times. CONTRADICTION IN TERMS.

Sir Christopher Wren, the great English architect who rebuilt so many of the London churches after the fire of London in 1666, said that a preacher could only be conveniently heard in a galleried church seated for not more than 2,000 people and that the voice will not carry more than 50 feet in front of a pulpit, 30 feet on either side and 20 feet behind. There is considerable truth in this as the Reformers found in the larger churches, none of which had been built with any idea of people hearing sermons in any part of the building other than the central space of the nave. Accordingly, where there was no parish church in a cathedral town, for instance, only a convenient part of the great church was retained for use, such as choirs of Dunkeld and Dunblane, while in such places as St. Andrews and Elgin where there was already a parish church the cathedral was allowed to go to ruin. No one could have any use for such churches then, and in any case the revenues which maintained them were alienated to people who, in modern phrase, 'couldn't care less'. It was the same with the great town churches; in the smaller places, such as Linlithgow, the eastern part was partitioned off for use and the rest remained empty, but, all praise to their Town Council, maintained. Haddington fared worse: they used the nave there but today the choir and transepts are in ruin. In the larger

39

burghs such as Edinburgh, Stirling, Perth, Dundee and Aberdeen the great churches were divided among two or more separate congregations. The aisles were filled with lofts and the pulpit was placed in a convenient central position irrespective of what the previous arrangement had been. It was all practical enough and made the best of a difficult job. Large Gothic churches with numerous chapels and arcades were built for other purposes, and it is wishful thinking to imagine that they can ever be good Presbyterian preaching churches.

Little was done or, in fact, could be done about building new kirks for the first fifty or sixty years after 1560. There were plenty of old churches in various states of repair to patch up and use in the manner described. The first church of any importance to be erected was at Burntisland in 1592. The medieval kirk, whose ruins may still be seen to the north of the town, was abandoned, doubtless because it was too small and rather far away, so the present building was placed within the burgh, above the sea. It is somewhat revolutionary, being square on plan with tower supported by four great arches rising through the middle, a shallow gallery runs round the outside walls and the pulpit stands against one of the square tower piers. The gallery and canopied magistrates pew (previously the castle seat) opposite the pulpit date from the 17th century, and the upper part of the tower from 1750, but the general conception is undoubtedly that of 1592. Sundry authorities have tried to puzzle out the origin of the design but no satisfactory conclusion has been reached. The tradition that it is copied from the North Church in Amsterdam, built later than Burntisland and of totally different plan, can hardly be accurate! After all, there is nothing very strange about the architectural detail: it is merely the shape which is curious, and it is perfectly conceivable that this is due to the reasoning of some logical Scot, tired of the unsatisfactory conversions of Popish kirks, trying to work out a better plan for the Reformed rite. Be that as it may, the experiment was not repeated in quite that form, for in general new churches were to carry on the pre-Reformation tradition, so far as the structure was concerned, and were gradually to develop from that.

Apart from lack of finance, the small amount of building carried out for the fifty years after the Reformation may be accounted for by the uneasy situation of the Church. Knox died in 1572 and the virtual leadership passed to Andrew Melville, who was somewhat more austere than his predecessor. Meanwhile a curious sort of Episcopacy was introduced—unconsecrated bishops were appointed who drew their revenue for the commendators and remained mere cyphers themselves. This, largely political, policy was abandoned in 1592 and a Presbyterian regime followed till 1610 when James VI, now also King of England, imposed a more normal type of Episcopacy. Three ministers went south to be consecrated in London. Whatever opinions may be held about Episcopacy its establishment undoubtedly had a settling influence from the building point of view, and this being a very material matter involving pounds, shillings and pence, it is difficult to avoid the inference that people accepted the policy as reasonably secure. James VI understood the Scottish character a great deal better than he is generally given credit for, and had his

son Charles I been as shrewd it is conceivable that there
might have been no further change to this day. Be that
as it may, the building of kirks was restarted and one of
the first was the largest since the Reformation and for a
long time to come, namely, Greyfriars in Edinburgh.
In 1561 the Town Council of Edinburgh had petitioned
for the use of the gardens formerly belonging to the
Greyfriars as a burial place for the town. This was
granted, but 'church extension' became urgent and in
1612 the Old Greyfriars was begun, that is the eastern
part of the present church. No church of any size,
excepting Burntisland, had been erected since the masons
had been at work on the choirs of Stirling and Linlithgow nearly a hundred years previously, and further,
nothing comparable in scale had been built in England
for at least eighty years. Even so, Greyfriars carried on
the Gothic tradition of form and plan. It consisted of a
rectangle set approximately east and west with lean-to
aisles divided from the central space by arcades of six
bays: in fact, just the plan of the nave of a large medieval
church. Now, though the Scottish Church was in
government Episcopalian, the form of service and the
arrangement for worship worked out since the Reformation remained much as before. The pulpit was the
central feature and accordingly it was set in the centre,
against the middle pillar of the south arcade. There was
no question of an altar at the east end, for there was a
doorway under the east window which, though built
up, may still be seen. The architectural details are
extremely simple: plain octagonal piers supported
pointed arches and galleries were built across the end
gables—all facing the central pulpit and the space for the

tables in front of it. There was a tower at the west end, but from Gordon of Rothiemay's bird's-eye view of Edinburgh in 1647 it appears to have been rather insignificant. Though simple enough, the scale of this church was imposing, for it is roughly the same size as the nave of Glasgow Cathedral and far bigger than that of St. Giles' in Edinburgh. The church later fell on troubled times, for its tower was used as a powder magazine and blew up. The ruins of the west end were patched and in 1718 another church called New Greyfriars was added. In 1938 the dividing wall between these two churches was removed in order to make one kirk, an interesting experiment, though it cannot be called a 'restoration' or 'putting back', for they had never been intended to be a unit.

A smaller example was begun in the same year, 1612, at Dirleton in East Lothian, to take the place of the Romanesque church at Gullane which had previously served the parish. Dirleton is a typical continuation of the long, narrow medieval plan employed for the country kirks, though it has a tower at the west end which was rare before the Reformation. As at Greyfriars the windows and other details tend towards the retention of a simple Gothic motif. A south aisle was added in 1664, during the second Episcopacy, by the laird of Archerfield. This is by far the most ornamental part of the building and is a curious combination of Gothic and classical detail. The interior of this church has been altered out of all recognition.

Other churches of this period which are still in use are Cawdor, dating from 1619, with a picturesque tower; South Queensferry, a simple rectangle, rather wider for

43

its length than normal, which was consecrated by Bishop Lindsay of Edinburgh in 1635; and Careston in Angus, a charming little kirk of 1636. The two last mentioned were erected for new parishes formed at the time. Long narrow churches which have been abandoned, but which are tolerably complete except for the roof, may be found at Longside in Aberdeenshire which was built by the Earl Marischal in 1620, at Anworth in Kirkcudbright-shire and at Durness in Sutherland (1619).

There is little doubt that these churches were all arranged with a pulpit central on the south wall and conformed very much with the plan earlier adapted by the Presbyterian party. There is, however, an interesting exception in the kirk of Dairsie in Fife. Archbishop Spottiswood of St. Andrews, who lived in the adjoining castle, built a new church in 1621. He was influenced by the liturgical movement in England, for it is recorded that a screen surmounted by the Royal arms was provided, and the inference is that there was an altar at the east end. Though these features did not last long, the fabric survives. It is a simple rectangular building with curious Gothic windows and a quaint belfry perched on the south-west corner with the aid of complicated corbelling. The roof was originally flat and surrounded by a parapet, but this has been altered.

An interesting city church, at the Tron in Edinburgh, was begun in 1637 to the design of John Mylne, King's Master Mason, in his capacity of Master of Works to the town. It took a long time to build, for it was not in use for another ten years and since then it has suffered various indignities and mishaps. When first erected it was laid out on what may be called the T-plan; that is, the main body of the kirk is the normal rectangle but to afford more seating accommodation an extra aisle or wing was built opposite the pulpit. In the case of the Tron the aisle was removed to form Hunter Square and the body of the kirk was shortened one bay at either end about 1790 when the South Bridge was formed. Its picturesque steeple was burnt in the great fire of 1824 and replaced to another design in 1828. The fire, however, did not damage the curtailed kirk, which is still spanned by its original oak roof. The walls are treated with a quaint version of early Renaissance pilasters but the window tracery is still influenced by Gothic.

Apart from complete kirks there are numerous interesting fragments and parts of buildings which survive from the period of the first Episcopacy. For instance, the minister of Cupar in Fife, William Scott, built an extra storey on to the 15th-century tower and crowned it with a picturesque balustrade and spire in 1620. Indeed Fife is notable for its steeples, which are of a type peculiar to the county. They derive their inspiration from 15th-century examples such as those of the Town Kirk and St. Salvator's in St. Andrews and may be found at Pittenweem, Anstruther Easter and Largo. Another good steeple of the period with medieval ancestry is that of the Tron Kirk in Glasgow, which is similar to that of the Cathedral.

Aberdeenshire too was evolving a local speciality in the shape of very elaborate belfries. Few of these belfries adorn the churches for which they were built, but being comparatively small and their workmanship being so good, they tended to be carefully taken down and re-erected if the old kirk was demolished and a new

one built. The 1636 belfry at Leslie now adorns the
west gable of its third church, which was built in 1815.
Other examples of these fine belfries may be seen at
Insch (1613), Gartly (1621), Clatt (1640), Drumblade
(1641), St. Fergus (1644) and a double one at Turriff.

The bells which hung in these towers and belfries are
also interesting. As with church building, there is a thin
period after the Reformation, but from the beginning
of the 17th century many contemporary examples are
to be found, for bells appeared to be just as important
to the Protestant church as they were to the Catholic.
Further, it is curious to note that their times of ringing
carried on, unwittingly no doubt, the hours of Catholic
worship in many parishes till the early years of this
century. It was common to find the bell rung daily at
an early hour in the morning which marked the Angelus
and in the evening which perpetuated the close of the
day with the 'de profundis'. The Sunday ringings were
more elaborate. Most parishes had only one bell which,
if early 17th century, was probably imported from the
Netherlands. The Burgerhuys family of Middelburg is
responsible for the call to worship in many parishes to
this day. Jan, the first member who concerns us, provided bells for Melrose (1608), Maxton (1609), Earlston,
Fyvie (1609) and Lundie (1617). He was succeeded by
his son Michael, who supplied bells at Ancrum (1618),
Stitchell (1632), South Queensferry (1635), Leslie (1642),
Peterhead (1642), Coul (1646) and Smailholm (1647), to
mention but a few. There was also Andreas Ehem whose
bells survive at Roscobie (1620) and Strichen (1633),
Peter Jansen with bells at Midmar (1642), Glenbuchat,
Rathen (1643) and Auchterless (1644). Later was Peter

Ostens of Rotterdam whose bells are at Banchory Ternan (1664) and Carriden (1674). There were, besides the Dutchmen, several Edinburgh founders working during the century such as George Hog, James Monteith, John Meikle and Robert Maxwell. Their bells may be found in many parts of the country.

At the Reformation most of the church plate had either been carried away or destroyed as being too closely associated with the central act of Catholic worship. It is obvious that this deficiency cannot have been made good, for it is significant to find an Act of Parliament of 1617 which ordains 'that all the Paroch Kirks within this Kingdom to be provided with Bafins and Lavoirs for the ministration of the Sacrament of Baptifme; and of Cups, Tables and Table-Cloathes, for the ministration of the Holy Communion'.

Throughout the 17th century kirks were acquiring new communion cups from various sources and of various types, thus providing the country with a magnificent heritage of the work of the silversmiths of Edinburgh, Glasgow and other places.

The mention of basins and lavers for baptism is worthy of note, for it indicates the normal reformed practice in Scotland from the 16th century till recent times. The medieval fonts were cast out and baptism was conducted from a basin of silver or pewter attached by a wrought-iron bracket to the pulpit. Unfortunately the bracket tradition has largely died out, though many of the basins remain in use hidden in modern pedestals of stone or wood. Brackets occasionally remain attached to pulpits as at Pencaitland, but the finer ones are generally to be found in museums.

Woodwork of the early 17th century is rarely to be found; there was much of it and from what remains the quality was good. One of the earliest and most attractive pieces is the little pulpit from Partan in Kirkcudbrightshire which is dated 1598 and is now in the Museum of Antiquities in Edinburgh. It is of Gothic type with a sounding board inscribed 'FEIR THE LORD AND HONOUR HIS HOUS'. Pencaitland has an old pulpit and some typically Jacobean pew fronts. The grand pulpit in St. Salvator's College Kirk, St. Andrews, came from the Town Kirk and though it has lost its sounding board it still retains its lectern and its hour-glass bracket. This last feature, like the baptismal bracket, was a common one on all pulpits of the 17th and 18th centuries. The hour glass was turned at the beginning of the sermon and probably ran through several times before the end of the discourse. It is very rare to find them still attached to pulpits, but several are preserved in museums and other places.

The unfortunate policy of Charles I in forcing a new service book upon the Church in 1637 led to the drawing up of the National Covenant and the disestablishment of Episcopacy in 1638. It is curious, though, that this book was the first to be drawn up in Scotland for Scotland. The Roman Liturgy was probably never used, for Scottish cathedrals adopted variations of the rites of Sarum or Lincoln. The early Reformers also used an English book, namely the Prayer Book of Edward VI. This was but for a short period, for it was quickly followed by Knox's book prepared for Geneva. It will be seen, therefore, that though elaborate ceremonies were absent, worship in Scotland had a liturgical background and Knox's book was the basis of this till the attempted introduction of the ill-fated 1637 book. The reaction to it was very violent and drove the Kirk into the Puritan influence from England for the next two hundred and fifty years.

The return to Presbyterianism, however important it may have been from the political point of view, meant very little from the building point of view for, in general, the requirements for worship were the same. So it follows that kirks continued to be built on the same lines, only not so many were built. The reason is simple enough, for the country was in a disturbed state, a condition seldom conducive to building. Meanwhile in London the Westminster Assembly of Divines was discussing a policy and basic order for a Presbyterian establishment not only for Scotland, but for England and Ireland as well. The enactments formulated by this predominantly English body came to be, and still are, the tenets of the Scottish Church. From it came the Confession of Faith, the Catechisms, the metrical Psalms and the Directory of Public Worship: in fact all that so many people now regard as solely Scottish forms of worship.

The ensuing execution of Charles I in 1649 and the defeat of Charles II in 1651 by Cromwell led to an external suppression of Presbyterian government, for, during the Commonwealth, the General Assembly was not allowed to meet and the army 'Independants' were a considerable nuisance to everyone.

Nevertheless in the troubled times between 1638 and the Restoration in 1660, a certain amount of church building was carried out. The Kirk of Yarrow was

49

erected in 1640 and Fenwick in 1643. By curious co-incidence both these churches were burnt down in comparatively recent times and since re-roofed. Fenwick unfortunately lost its contemporary pulpit during the fire. The large church of Kirkintilloch was built in 1644, but has been abandoned since 1913. During the same year the tiny church of Lyne in Peeblesshire was reconstructed. Its canopied pews are dated 1644 and its pulpit is also of that period.

Churches erected during the Commonwealth are still more unusual, but cases of necessity arose as a result of it. The people of Ayr had worshipped in the medieval church of St. John, which stood slightly apart from the town on a site which Cromwell's officers requisitioned for a fort. Accordingly it was barred to the parishioners and they were forced to build a new church in 1654. It is a large T-plan kirk which boasted one of the finest pulpits in Scotland. In 1887 the claims of an organ were considered to have a priority on the pulpit site and so most of it was removed, but in 1951 it was replaced again as nearly as possible. The grand lofts of the Trades, the Merchants and the Sailors remain untouched and make an impressive interior.

The church at Cramond was rebuilt in 1656, but has been so much added to and altered that few features of that date remain. Three years later the now ruined church at North Berwick was started to replace the medieval kirk near the harbour which had become a 'totall ruine'. The foundations of the latter have recently been uncovered.

The Restoration of Charles II in 1660 brought in its train the Second Episcopacy and, as with the First

Episcopacy, there was a revival of church building which produced some very interesting structures. In spite of the re-establishment of bishops there was no attempt to alter the form of worship or the organisation of Kirk Sessions and Presbyteries, so, as with the previous changes of ecclesiastical government one way or another, there was no new requirement in the planning of churches.

Eckford and Cavers in Roxburghshire, built in 1662 and 1663 respectively, were two of the first to be erected under the new regime. The former was a plain rectangle to which a charming classic north aisle, dated 1724, was added by the Bennets of Marlfield. The latter, incorporating some medieval work, is larger and shows strong Gothic tradition in the traceried window of the north aisle which pertained to the Elliots of Stobs. This church was abandoned when a new one was built in 1822 and a few years later converted into a school. Bowden in the same county contains some excellent work of the 1660s, including a particularly fine laird's loft of the Kerrs of Cavers. Unfortunately efforts to medievalise this church earlier in the present century have altered its character. Glencorse in Midlothian, dated 1665, with the Woodhouselee aisle on the south side dated 1697 and its little shingled spire, must have been a lovely church amid romantic surroundings. However, it is fast going to ruin as it was abandoned in 1885 when a new church was built. The Gothic forms carried on for a few more years as may be seen at Tulliallan in Fife and the fragment at Logie in Stirlingshire dated 1684. The church for the newly formed parish of Tulliallan, which had been disjoined from

Culross, was built in 1675. Having been abandoned when a new church was built in 1833 it is unfortunately roofless, though otherwise reasonably intact. It is a good example of a T-plan church of that period, with obvious provision for the pulpit on the centre of the south wall, for traceried Gothic windows are arranged in such a way that they lit lofts in the north, east and west ends of the T. There is also an elegant tower with some classic detail.

Not all the churches of the period conformed to pattern, however, and perhaps this may be more as a result of the emerging status of the architect as we know him today than of actual requirements. For instance, a very curious and unique church was built at Lauder in 1673 which is attributed to Sir William Bruce, undoubtedly our most eminent architect of the period, who designed Holyroodhouse and who was largely responsible for the introduction of the developed Renaissance to Scotland. This church carries 'central planning' a step further than the T, for it has four arms of equal size forming a Greek cross with a tower in the centre. The upper part of the tower is octagonal and is capped by a short slated spire. The four arms of the cross are very narrow and each contains a loft to which access is obtained by outside or fore-stairs.

Another unique and very different church is that of the Canongate, which was begun in 1688 by the order of James VII with the Royal Overseer of Works, James Smith, as architect. It is a large building whose plan is inspired by Continental Baroque rather than by anything in Scotland. It has a nave with aisles, shallow transepts and a chancel with an apse beyond. How it

DURISDEER, DUMFRIESSHIRE

The Queensberry tomb, 1711

KILBIRNIE, AYRSHIRE

The Garnock loft, early 18th century

was arranged in those days is not known. It certainly could never have been suitable for either Episcopacy or Presbyterianism in the 17th century though it admirably meets the demands of the worship of today. Apart from its plan, Canongate is full of interest, for it is one of the first churches with a special street front of wrought stone, while the sides and back are rubble, harled. This device became common enough later on, but at that date it is another pointer to foreign Baroque influence. The street gable is curvilinear of the simpler Dutch manner and the windows are round-headed except in the apse where there is a strange Gothic window. Before the Canongate was finished James VII had gone and the spirited Royal Arms high on the gable are those of William of Orange.

The Revolution Settlement of 1690 restored Presbyterianism and the findings of the Westminster Divines were confirmed. Again this was important politically, but as far as the average kirk was concerned it made not a bit of difference. The requirements for worship were just the same and accordingly churches continued to be built the same way. For instance, Gladsmuir was made a parish in 1695 and the kirk erected at that time is of the typical rather narrow T-plan with crow-stepped gables and a western belfry. In arrangement there is nothing to distinguish it from, say, Tulliallan of the Episcopacy or Yarrow of the earlier Presbyterian regime. Unfortunately Gladsmuir is now a ruin, having been abandoned for a later church near by.

The 17th century ends with one of its most outstanding kirks remotely situated in the hills of Dumfriesshire, namely Durisdeer, built in 1699. The body of the kirk is based on a simple T-plan, but to the north, screened by a wrought-iron grille, is a square aisle containing the exuberant monument to the Duke of Queensberry dated 1711; a mortuary chapel in the grand style with profusion of black and white marble, barley-sugar columns and fleeting cherubs. Attached to the kirk on the west is a square building, which was formerly the school, with a high balustraded tower rising out of the middle of it. This portion is now disused, but the whole fabric is one of the most important monuments in Scotland.

To end the account of 17th-century work with commendation is not so curious as it may seem. It was a century fraught with difficulties and with violently contending passions, yet a vast amount was done in spite of surrounding disturbances and remarkably low funds for church purposes. A significant plan was evolved which suited the worship of either party and, though it is often misunderstood today by the Church which gave birth to it, there is still time for careful reflection. The Roman Church on the Continent, more alive, we must admit, to prevailing tendencies, is building churches on lines which should make us ashamed of giving up our traditional arrangements for those of 'Gothic revival' Anglicanism. The centrality of plan conceived in the 17th century is a vigorous witness of the Reformed teaching which was also adopted in a different manner by the Roman counter-Reformation. As far as architectural style was concerned, it may be noted that Gothic forms lingered throughout the period. There was no 17th-century Gothic revival. The Gothic mannerism did not die out till the end of the century, for it was the normal way to build unless something special was erected by some prominent master mason who had heard of the Renaissance, and then Renaissance detail there was. The Tron Kirk in Edinburgh has classical pilasters framing Gothic windows. But that was in the capital—in the country building was more traditional, though many kirks were so plain and functional that it is hard to say which influence was at work. Internal furnishings were often elaborate; carved pulpits and lecterns, fine laird's lofts and monuments made bright and charming interiors.

Just because the conception of a church built for a new rite was utterly different to the medieval, it did not follow that it lacked all artistic interest.

## THE EIGHTEENTH CENTURY:
## THE THEME AND VARIATIONS

IT has been stressed that the parish in medieval days was sorely pressed for funds and as a result that the parish church of that period was not likely to be a very grand building. It has also been mentioned that certain of the churches before and after the Reformation were paid for by pious benefactors, but nothing so far has been said of the ordinary post-Reformation method of financing the building of kirks. In all but certain burgh parishes, where the Town Council was responsible for their church or churches, the landowners of the parish held the church, churchyard and manse in trust for the parishioners. In some cases there might only be one landowner, in others many, but as owners they were responsible for the maintenance of the church and the manse and for the provision of new ones when necessary. These landowners were known as heritors. It is obvious that the heritors would not be particularly keen to disburse more money than was required, especially should they happen to be Roman Catholics or Episcopalians, and so church maintenance was not of the highest order. Further, when it was estimated that a new church would cost a few pounds less to provide than to repair the existing one, more often than not the old kirk was left to ruin and a new one was built. This is one of the reasons why so few medieval churches remain in Scotland. When the heritors did build a new church they had to provide a certain number of seats, which in landward parishes were divided among their tenants. Seating plans for their allocation may be found occasionally, there is one at Kirkliston; frequently, as at Crail, the country house or farm names were painted on the pews. In order to economise in space, hence in the total bulk of the building, these seats were liable to be crammed together as closely as possible—giving only just enough space to sit and stand. Kneeling, not being a position adopted by the congregation in a Scottish church, did not require to be provided for. Hence it is to be found that the churches of the 18th century, as their fore-runners of the 17th, are very compact. There was no regard to the merits of open space within and seldom much for elaboration without, except in towns where it was considered proper that the church should be an ornament to the streets.

The early part of the 18th century is not remarkable for a great number of kirks. The Union with England in 1707 had not been a blessing to the country financially and there was a certain stagnation of national life as a result of it. However, by the 60's and 70's of the century a great revival took place. The enlightened policy of the improving lairds, often bitterly opposed by their conservative tenants, revolutionised agriculture, and the rural population increased rapidly. This meant in many places that the old churches became too small, and so by the end of the century new ones were being built all over the country.

From the architectural point of view Gothic detail had

to all intents and purposes vanished by the end of the 17th century and the new kirks, when in any way embellished, followed classical forms. The plan with its central pulpit remained the same as before, but, for the greater ease of speaking, the church tended to grow shorter and wider.

One of the earliest essays of the new century was the rebuilding of Polwarth in Berwickshire in 1703. It is a simple T-plan building, possibly standing on medieval foundations, with a western tower and short slated spire. The southern façade has a doorway at each end and one in the middle, behind the pulpit, for the minister. Between these doorways are windows and inscribed panels. It is very complete and straight-forward with charming details.

The 18th century was a period of transition. The old feudal ways were vanishing and the intimate society of the dependants clustering round the castle of their lord was being broken up. This was largely because the lord wanted more elbow-room and to emulate the spacious parks and vistas of his southern neighbours. He had often, therefore, to move the village which clustered round his house and to rebuild both house and village. This of course was generally to the advantage not only of lord and tenant, but of us today. The trees in the pleasant parks have grown to maturity and form a characteristic feature of our landscape, while the new 'planned' villages have given us the charming semi-rural Gifford, the miniature county town of Inveraray, the severely laid out Fochabers and so forth. The first of these removals which resulted in a good church was at Yester, where the Second Marquess of Tweeddale laid out the village of Gifford.

Its church was built in 1710 to close the vista of the main street and fulfils this function very admirably. In plan it is the usual T with the long side set opposite the street, but to break the line a tower, capped by a solid parapet and short slated spire, projects in the middle. It would be difficult to find a more seemly church anywhere, suitable both for its purpose of worship and as an ornament to the village. Though the tower is rather medieval in spirit the general feeling of the whole is Renaissance. The flickering Gothic of the previous century has gone except for an odd pointed window in the gable. Carrington, Midlothian, erected in 1711, is similar to Gifford and also includes a small tower standing out from the southern façade.

In 1712 the imposing tower at Greenlaw was built as the town prison. The church extends eastwards from it and formerly there was a court-house to the west. It is an unusual and interesting composition.

Simple but charming churches of this period, generally of the T-plan, are to be found scattered up and down the country, such as Elie in Fife (1726), Orwell in Kinross-shire (1729), Newbattle in Midlothian (1727), Glasserton in Wigtownshire (1732), Livingston in West Lothian (1733), New Spynie in Moray (1736), Kinneff in Kincardineshire (1738), Oxnam in Roxburghshire (1738), Golspie in Sutherland (1738) and Reay in Caithness (1739). Of these perhaps Golspie is the least altered. Outside it is very simple with white harled walls and square-headed sash and case-windows. Within the old arrangements remain, the grand contemporary pulpit with its carved sounding board, the long communion table extending down the centre of the church, the old lofts, the latter including the splendidly carved and panelled seat of the Duke of Sutherland in the aisle. Such a church in such a condition is a far more valuable part of the national heritage than many a so-called 'restored' medieval church.

Besides these excellent examples of well-proportioned rural churches, built in most cases by local masons, there arose some rather more pretentious buildings. At Hamilton the medieval church was alongside the Palace, so, in order to gain more privacy, the Duke of the day built a new church in 1732 at the other side of the town with a street leading axially up to its main door under the tower. This church was designed by William Adam, senior, on rather a peculiar plan. The centre of the church is circular and from it project four arms, like the outline of a Celtic cross. The whole style is of course strictly classical.

Another good classical composition is the tower which was added to the medieval church of St. Ninian's (Stirling) in 1734. The church was blown up in 1746 and only fragments remain, but the tower stands and might resemble an Italian campanile had not the harling been mistakenly removed from its walls.

In 1739 a very noble church, St. Andrew's, was begun in Glasgow to the design of Allan Dreghorn. It took a long time to build, for it was not completed till 1756, but it was the first of the large town churches in the grand classical manner. On the west is a great Corinthian portico and the pilastered side elevations are capped by balustrades and urns. The simple rectangular plan bears a certain resemblance to St. Martin-in-the-Fields, London (1722–6), which was a church much copied at the time.

The interior of St. Andrew's is divided into aisles, containing mahogany-fronted galleries, supported by elegant Corinthian columns. There is also some fine plaster work. This building must be regarded as opening a new epoch for town churches.

Another large burgh church was erected in 1755 in Aberdeen to the plans of James Gibbs, who designed St. Martin-in-the-Fields just mentioned. Gibbs was a native of Aberdeen and not only was this his last work but, so far as is known, his only building in Scotland. The problem here was not that of a new church on a new site, but the rebuilding of the nave of the great medieval parish church of St. Nicholas. This large church had been subdivided after the Reformation, and Gibbs had to fit his building on to the medieval central tower and transepts. In plan the new church followed its predecessor in having lean-to aisles but it was rather shorter. The exterior is very simple, of finely wrought ashlar masonry, and the interior is also very direct with substantial square piers supporting heavy arches. It has a gallery all round with the canopied seat of the Lord Provost at the east end and the splendid pulpit stands against a pier in the middle of the south arcade. This interior is one of the finest in Scotland though unfortunately darkened by the later insertion of coloured glass.

In the country the more traditional plan was still in vogue. Auldearn (Nairnshire), built in 1757, is very narrow and very long; so much so that the minister writing some eighty years later says, 'The length is completely out of proportion to the breadth'. This may be partly accounted for by the fact that it is built on medieval foundations. The ruins of the medieval choir are still standing to the east.

Kilmany in Fife, built in 1768, is also very traditional and quite delightful with its white walls and simple astragaled windows. Alves in Moray, built a year later, is similar, though larger, and unfortunately has been abandoned within recent years. Inverarity (1754) in Angus, Drumblade (1773) and Migvie (1777) in Aberdeenshire, Cabrach (1786) in Banffshire, Ardoch (1780) in Perthshire and Rogart (1771) in Sutherland, are all good examples of this type, but perhaps the best are Cromarty and Glenbuchat. The former is a fair-sized T-plan kirk and the latter a small rectangular building, now disused. It is very complete, however, with its painted pulpit and loft, cobbled floor and box pews.

The towns were beginning to strike out on a different line, though it is true that the High Kirk in Inverness (1772) is a large edition of the T-plan with a fine tower. On the other hand, Penicuik (1771) has a Doric portico. Lanark put up a great barn, almost square, in 1777, which is relieved by a decent tower facing the street. Cupar in Fife replaced most of its medieval church by a bulky rectangle in 1785. These wide, almost square plans, enabled the wing or aisle opposite the pulpit to be dispensed with, and the gallery to run round three walls of the interior in a horseshoe or semi-octagonal outline. In the same year Strathmiglo, near Cupar, built a church somewhat similar though on a much smaller scale. An early rural example of the wider plan in the same district is at Cults (1793), which unlike the two previously mentioned is reasonably untouched by the church furnisher or stained glass purveyor.

Further north, Montrose in 1791 built an immense unadorned edifice, but the interior is a fascinating example of a church with two tiers of galleries (the only example left), giving possible accommodation for 3,000 people. Outside, a very beautiful Gothic revival tower and spire were added to the street façade in 1832 to the design of James Gillespie Graham.

A town church at the other end of the country forms an interesting contrast. It is Inveraray, begun in 1796 to the design of Robert Mylne, in the charming little whitewashed capital of Argyll, a planned town laid out for the same reason as Gifford, namely to replace the older town which was too near the ducal castle. The church is placed in the middle of the main street which is widened into a square to receive it. Most unfortunately the central steeple, which gave not only a finish to the church but was the focal point of the whole town design, was removed in 1941. Appeals for its replacement are being made. The reason why the steeple was central may not be obvious at first sight, but it stood on a wall which divides the building into two churches— one for English services, the other for Gaelic. The interiors of both have been entirely refurnished.

Still another example of a planned town of the period which provided an admirable site for its kirk is Fochabers. This community was removed from the vicinity of Gordon Castle, and on the south side of the square of the new town a grand kirk was built for the parish of Bellie in 1798. This kirk, designed by John Baxter of Edinburgh, was very properly, as at Inveraray, the dominating architectural feature of the town, which it still remains. A classical portico, surmounted by a good steeple flanked by symmetrical houses on either side, makes a noteworthy composition emphasising the undoubted status of the Establishment.

At Kingussie (1792) and Kirkhill (1799) in Invernessshire, and Little Dunkeld (1798) in Perthshire, may be seen simple straightforward renderings of these wide kirks. They are unaffected and sincere though their bulk makes them rather ungainly, hence not as attractive aesthetically as the narrower churches earlier in the century. They do, however, compare favourably with many of the Gothic churches which were to follow.

Besides the simple expedient of widening churches there were experiments made, some no doubt mere flights of fancy on the part of the architect, others possibly an endeavour to obtain the most compact plan possible with a view to every sitter being within the shortest possible distance of the pulpit. The first effort in this line was the only circular plan of the century for the parish of Kilarrow at Bowmore in the Isle of Islay. A stunted but charming classical steeple stands at the head of the main street, and behind it the gleaming white circular kirk capped by a conical slated roof. Over the door is a Latin inscription which may be rendered, 'For the study of Piety, and the culture of Truth and Honour, Daniel Campbell, Lord of this Island, built this church at his own charges and dedicated it to the Supreme Deity in the year 1767'.

The next experiment of this sort was at Kelso in 1773 when a large octagonal church was constructed for a congregation of 3,000. There is another octagonal church at Dreghorn in Ayrshire built in 1788, and a third was erected at Eaglesham in Renfrewshire by the

Earl of Eglintoun in 1790. This last has been extended, so is no longer octagonal. Others later were in the adjoining parishes of Glenorchy and Kilmorich in Argyll dated 1811 and 1824, respectively, but both are in the early Gothic revival style then fashionable.

There was also a venture into the oval in Edinburgh. St. Andrew's, George Street, the first church in the New Town, was started in 1785 as the result of a competition won by Major Frazer of the Engineers. The chief external features, namely the elegant steeple and Corinthian portico, were added in 1789 to the design of William Sibbald. The steeple is notable for containing the first ring of 8 bells to be installed in Scotland on the English model. These bells were cast by William and Thomas Mears of London in 1788.

Another unusual plan was at Lasswade when in 1794 a square church was built with shallow extensions on each side, thus making a Greek cross. Through neglect of maintenance this interesting church became so ruinous that it was recently pulled down. This is sad, the more so as a former minister writes of the 'church just now erecting, which in point of accommodation, and magnificence of structure, will far exceed any modern country church in Scotland'.

The 18th century was classical as far as style went, and towards the end of the period the plan broadened out, producing in some cases roof spans over 60 feet. This was desirable from a practical point of view and made possible by the import of heavy timbers. These churches were the logical development of the Reformed arrangement, and alterations to those remaining untouched should not be undertaken lightly. Too frequently in the past their unique character has been destroyed by the misguided enthusiasm of those who would follow the precedents of the 19th-century Anglicans without fully understanding their own tradition. True, the services for which they were designed were of English puritan origin, but the buildings themselves are purely Scottish.

# THE NINETEENTH CENTURY:
# AN AGE OF REVIVALS

THE turn of the century marks the tentative beginnings of the Gothic revival from which, even now, a hundred and sixty years later, we have hardly extricated ourselves. During the first ten or fifteen years the honours between the classical and Gothic were fairly equally divided and then the fashionable new and romantic style 'walked away with it', leaving the classical to linger in the Grecian terraces of Edinburgh and some other towns. Though this change of style was largely brought about by a literary awakening of interest in medieval romance, which was to produce the writings of Sir Walter Scott, it did not change the plan and arrangement of the Scottish Kirk. Thus the earlier results were often unsatisfactory unless frankly naïve. Real Gothic architecture had been a dynamic, functional style, not something applied, as this was, often in an English Perpendicular form which, except for the tracery of an odd window, had never before been seen in Scotland.

There are plenty of examples of the early 19th century, for church building was still on the boom, Scotland had never been so prosperous or so populous before. Agriculture was flourishing, not only because of the improvements, but owing to the necessities of the Napoleonic

War and, though the Industrial Revolution had hardly started, there was considerable commercial prosperity around Glasgow, so it is little wonder that conditions were ideal for building. Towns were extending to double their former size, great farm steadings were being erected all over the low country and the Church had to keep pace. Medieval churches were abandoned or pulled down in great numbers, without a second thought, and new buildings were substituted. It is to this period, a decade or two before and after 1800, that Scotland owes the large majority of the churches in her older parishes.

Classical churches during the first ten years of the century include Dingwall with slight Gothic tendencies (1801), Fraserburgh (1802), Peterhead (1803), Inveresk (1803) and Ceres (1806). The last named is probably the most interesting internally, for its gallery and pews are all as originally fitted, including a most ingenious arrangement for setting up a couple of long communion tables through a series of box pews. All are of a fair size, particularly Peterhead, which was designed to seat 1,800, and all have pleasant spires, that of Fraserburgh being built at a cost of about £300 raised by public subscription.

In Aberdeenshire there are some delightful small kirks, several of which seem to have been directed by the same mind. Echt, built in 1804, is the largest, but Kildrummy (1805) and Bourtie (1806) are more perfectly preserved internally. These are both tiny, but although Kildrummy is only 37 feet by 33 feet inside it manages to have a narrow gallery round three walls. Their pointed windows are their only concession to

GLENBUCHAT, ABERDEENSHIRE

A simple 18th-century rural church

ST. ANDREW'S, GLASGOW

A grand 18th-century town church

Gothic and, fortunately, they still retain their clear glass and wooden astragals. Bourtie, one of the most unaltered interiors of its date, is now to all intents and purposes abandoned.

One of the earliest churches in a reasonably developed type of Gothic is Craig, near Montrose, which was built in 1799 at the expense of a patroness, Mrs. Ross of Rossie, and this may explain its surprising maturity and its high tower. The new church built at Kirkcaldy in 1807, on to the medieval tower, has a Gothic dress and it is amusing to note that at the time it was considered that it would be 'an ornament to the Town' were it not for the old tower! In fact counterfeit was preferred to the real thing built in the 15th century. A terrible accident occurred in this church in 1828 when the gallery fell and the ensuing panic caused 28 deaths. There was a similar panic at the old Laigh Kirk in Kilmarnock in 1801 without the gallery coming down! A piece of plaster fell from the ceiling as the people were assembling for the evening service; it was thought that the roof was collapsing and in the resulting confusion 29 people died. Owing to the apprehension caused by this disaster the heritors built a new church. Another fuss concerning the safety of a gallery, though without fatal consequences, led to a new church at Errol in 1830.

It is impossible to mention more than a few of the kirks erected during this period; their bulky form and stringy window tracery may be recognised throughout the country from Thurso to Whithorn, and many undoubtedly give cause to regret that the simple classic tradition was not maintained to produce more buildings of the delightful standard of Kilmaronock (1813) in

Dunbartonshire. However, by no means all the Gothic examples were mediocre. Occasionally one of the heritors might pay the difference between a 'plain' and an 'ornamented' kirk! This happened at Kincardine-in-Menteith where George Home Drummond of Blair Drummond made up the difference in 1814 and James Crichton, an Edinburgh architect, produced a very creditable building, arcaded and plaster-vaulted within, while outside is a western tower. Francis, Earl of Moray, gave the tower to the church of the adjoining parish of Kilmadock in 1823. This tower does much to hide a particularly ungainly kirk from the street of Doune, and it also serves as a reasonable landmark, so it is well justified. At Alloa a new church, designed by James Gillespie Graham, was built in 1819 with a fine Gothic spire about 200 feet high, while near by at Clackmannan (1817) and Airth (1820) the churches have considerable merit. Other typical Gothic examples of this period are Dunbar (1820), designed by James Gillespie Graham; Kilconquhar (1820), by R. & R. Dickson; St. David's, Ramshorn, Glasgow, by Thomas Rickman; and Kinnoul (1826), by William Burn. A significant point about the planning of these churches is that the pulpit was generally placed against an end or gable wall, not, as since the Reformation, on the long side. Otherwise, as they were very wide for their length, the plan was little affected and a gallery normally ran round three sides. Rather a novel plan, approximating to the old T-plan, was evolved by an Edinburgh architect, George Angus, who, apparently, was pleased with it, for Kinross (1832), Tulliallan (1833) and Kettle (1834) are all just the same. Another much more numerous series of similar kirks was designed by Thomas Telford, the famous engineer, and were known as the 'Parliamentary Churches'. These were constructed as a result of an Act of Parliament in 1824 providing a sum of nearly £55,000 for the provision of extra churches in the Highlands and Islands. By this means forty-three churches were built. Telford provided plans for a T-plan kirk and alternatives for a one- or two-storeyed manse. The church was a wide rectangle with the pulpit on the long side between two large windows, an aisle opposite, not always erected, and galleries. Perhaps Iona is one of the most often seen of these churches. Until some twenty years ago it was complete inside with its grand pulpit and long communion table. However, the interior is now without character and the pulpit is in the Folk Museum at Kingussie.

In Edinburgh some notable churches were being erected, such as St. George's, Charlotte Square (1911–1914), whose copper-covered dome designed by Robert Reid is the chief landmark of the New Town. William Burn's first work, at North Leith (1814–16), has a fine steeple and an excellent Ionic portico. In 1823 two large chapels-of-ease to St. Cuthbert's were erected, now the parish churches of Newington St. Leonard's (by Robert Brown) and St. Bernard's (by James Milne). Both have classic steeples and pilastered façades, the former retaining its original canopied pulpit. They were followed, the next year, by St. Mary's in the centre of Bellevue Crescent with a good Corinthian portico to the design of Thomas Brown. In Glasgow William Stark designed St. George's with an unusual and interesting steeple, while in Aberdeen John Smith built the clean-cut granite North Church in the Ionic order in 1826. In Elgin Archibald Simpson designed the present parish church which was opened in 1828 on the site of its medieval predecessor. It is a fine building with a Greek Doric portico at the west and at the east, a tower, which rises into a rendering of the choragic monument of Lysicrates in Athens. Also in 1828 was opened the extension church of Inverbrothock in Arbroath—a very severe exterior without spire or belfry, but within the Greek Revival galleries are worthy of note. In the country here and there a church was constructed which was free of the Gothic fancy dress and, as at Kilmaronock, the result is far more pleasing. Benholm (1832) in Kincardineshire is a case in point— very simple and very fitting.

About this period there was a considerable change in the method of partaking Communion which was to have a profound influence on the arrangement of church interiors. For over 250 years the people had come up to sit at the tables which were long and narrow with a bench on either side. After those partaking at the first 'table' had left, the second and following 'tables' were 'fenced' so the first group were normally outside the building. This was all right in country places, but as the towns increased it was soon found highly unsuitable to have large portions of the congregation in the street, and Dr. Chalmers is given the credit for introducing the custom of communicating in pews. It had been known in Elizabethan England and was forbidden by the General Assembly in 1825. Nevertheless, once started the custom stayed, and as a result one of the most characteristic features of the worship of the Church of

Scotland has all but vanished. The tables are remembered on Communion Sundays by the strips of linen fixed to the pews which represent the cloth formerly covering them, and perhaps descend from an even earlier strip of linen which in medieval days the clerks held across the altar steps as the people knelt to communicate there. The new custom did not make much impression on the church plan, though some table was essential from which the minister could conduct the service.

The arrangements which eventually obtained from this alteration in the form of worship were influenced by another factor, namely the invention of a new science called ecclesiology, which is the study of the use of churches, their shape and furnishings in relation to the liturgy carried on within them. Gothic gloom, stained glass, flickering of numerous candles, mysterious monks and so on had been made very thrilling by the romantic novel writers and poets of the time, and very good copy they were, but certain earnest people in England wanted to know more about it all. Nor was mere knowledge all they aspired to, but action so that the liturgy of the Book of Common Prayer could be celebrated in what, they considered, more seemly form in their ancient churches. Since the Reformation in that country the church plan had developed on different lines because the problem was different. To begin with, their medieval churches were larger than ours and generally had a much more clearly defined chancel. After various 16th- and 17th-century experiments the communion table came to be set against the east wall of the chancel on the site of the high altar, and the chancel itself tended to be treated as a place apart, used only by communicants during the communion service. Hence, as it was set aside for a separate purpose, many ancient rood screens were retained and are preserved to this day. The nave, on the other hand, was crammed with pews and galleries set round a pulpit placed in a reasonably central place. As here, their pulpits were very high and had smaller desks below. The pulpit itself was used for the sermon, the next stage down for reading the service, in the same way as our readers' 'letteroun', and the lowest stage was occupied by the parish clerk, who led the responses. Instrumental music was allowed, so an organ or sometimes a village orchestra was placed on a western gallery. New churches in England during the latter part of the 17th and 18th centuries normally had much shallower chancels than the long medieval ones, or none at all, and thus brought the table nearer the main bulk of the people—an idea which we had adopted at the outset though arranged differently.

This outline of the customs of another country may seem rather irrelevant, but as things were to turn out it is very pertinent. The ecclesiologists ignored the tendency towards a more central planning of churches. They thought that all churches should be based on a medieval plan with the long chancel, typical of England, without really grasping how the medieval people had used the church. They imagined that chancels should be filled with singers and the white-robed boys' choir was virtually their invention for parish churches. Having got the choir into the chancel the organ in most cases followed, and in the process not only were the spacious sanctuaries cluttered up with this instrument and numerous seats, but any number of fine Georgian organ cases were destroyed, together with numerous medieval screens in an attempt to open the building from end to end as it had never been opened before.

Again, this does not seem to have much to do with Scotland but, though the ecclesiologists were English, they sometimes mentioned Scotland in lectures and articles, and the invariable implication was that Scotland was a most barbarous and backward place as our new churches were built without chancels. Now the whole worship of the Church of Scotland had developed a direct central plan of profound significance. Chancels were regarded as an unnecessary appendage to a kirk— Scotland had planned along other lines and there was no functional use for a chancel except possibly to house the laird's loft. But although the jibes from the ecclesiologists in England did not make much outward impression to begin with, the time was ripe for developments and seeds of doubt sown from across the border did not fall on entirely unfertile ground.

The first results were external. Instead of the mere application of a few Gothic buttresses and a tower on to the walls of a normal plain kirk, ungainly though it might be, the whole outline was becoming far more English by the 1850's and 1860's. Spires whose ancestry might be traced to Norfolk or the Midlands rose in Aberdeenshire or Midlothian. The roof became steeply pitched as in the Early English or Decorated periods in the south, and often the general impression was that of a cruciform church with a long chancel. Inside, nothing had changed very much. The interior was probably arranged on the familiar old T-plan lines. Take the parish church of Stow, Midlothian, built in 1874, a fine

Gothic building with a lofty tower and spire attached to what appears to be a nave with a transept, and a chancel ending with an apse. The pulpit is opposite the transept or aisle and the apse contains a laird's seat—a most 'unecclesiological' arrangement!

As a result of the findings of a committee of enquiry into the adequacy of church accommodation, which was set up by the General Assembly in 1828, an enormous number of churches, particularly in towns, were built during this uneasy period of Gothic revival. This committee, with the celebrated Dr. Thomas Chalmers as its first convener, eventually became the Home Board. By aid of its grants some 600 churches were erected or enlarged before the end of the 19th century which, as may well be realised, is a very fair proportion of all the churches in Scotland. Another very active and, as it has turned out, unfortunate, source of church building was the Disruption. The reason for the Disruption in 1843 need not be stated here, and it is sufficient to say that 451 out of 1,203 ministers left the Establishment under the leadership of Dr. Chalmers to found the Free Church. This secession body built numerous churches, and within a few years most parishes in Scotland were provided with one. Owing to lack of funds most of the earlier examples were very simple and very dull from an architectural point of view, but their importance today is considerable and will be noted later.

The seed sown by the English ecclesiologists with regard to actual church building was nourished by another English movement of the early 19th century to which Scotland was not entirely immune, and whose moderated influence has done something to mould the

Church of today. This was the Tractarian or Oxford Movement which proclaimed the catholicity of the Church of England and which was instrumental in starting high church practices. Here a greater interest in the form and shape of services was the result, particularly with regard to praise. The psalm singing of the 18th century was incredibly dreary, and some abortive experiments were made in the direction of instrumental music, one of the pioneers in this and other practices being Dr. Lee of Old Greyfriars. At last in 1866 the General Assembly permitted the use of instrumental music in church, and the first hymnary was published in 1870. The Church Service Society was founded in 1865, and forms of service were published based on the old books of the Reformers. These movements coupled with the antiquarian researches of the ecclesiologists helped to alter the plans of churches, but nothing upset the average interior or retarded its orderly development more than the advent of the organ. The reaction in its favour was most alarming and in many places the organ was made the grand central feature, turning church interiors into caricatures of a concert hall—the religious significance all but vanished. It would be invidious to mention the names of one or two of the numerous kirks arranged as a result of this fashion, but it is as well to describe their general appearance, for it was in the 1870's, 80's and 90's that the churches in Scotland reached their lowest ebb, not only aesthetically but liturgically. Most of them are in built-up areas and have a façade of an elaborated version of English or French Decorated Gothic architecture facing the street. At one side is often a tower surmounted by a spire, the whole of the stone work is hard and metallic-looking and individual stones are sometimes raised into uneven lumps. An ornamented doorway, with the burning bush carved above it, opens into a dreary vestibule with crudely coloured tiles on the floor and a staircase at each end leading to the gallery. On going through one of the doorways into the kirk a stuffy smell, peculiar to Presbyterian Churches of this era, assails the visitor. (Anglican churches of these decades, whether north or south of the Border, have quite a different though equally distinctive smell.) In the body of the kirk the overwhelming impression is one of organ pipes and sticky varnish of a particularly devastating shade of dark brown. Narrow alleyways, paved with cast iron gratings, cut through a sea of varnished pews. These are sometimes set theatre fashion at angles, or in a semi-circle to face the organ and frequently the floor slopes gradually downward. The end wall is covered by the great instrument itself with rows of drab-coloured pipes held together by tortured bits of varnished woodwork standing on a podium of varnished panelling. In the midst of this strange composition is a rostrum or platform which can scarcely be dignified with the title of pulpit. This sorry affair is bracketed on to the instrument rather apologetically, it seems, as the 'vox humana' part of the performance. Anyhow it is a very decadent descendant of the splendid earlier pulpits with their grand sounding boards surmounted by golden doves— pulpits which really meant something and compelled attention to the Word even before the minister appeared. How can a platform attached to a large machine signify the teaching of the Reformed Church?

Below and in front of the organ is the organ console whose top is still used in some places as the communion table! Granted in most churches there is now a separate table for the celebration of the Sacrament, but as it is apt to be crammed between the organ console and the organ its effect and significance is nil. Such space as is left is often crowded with untidy chairs facing the people. For the choir is apt to sing at the people —another sign of the concert-hall influence.

This picture may seem overdrawn, but unfortunately it is a painfully true reflection on the state of hundreds of churches—so many, in fact, that congregations now tend to regard it as the correct Church of Scotland arrangement. The concert-house plan has had such a strong influence that it has resulted in the organ and choir becoming major, rather than subordinate, features of worship.

Long before the last of these astounding musical meeting-houses were built, thinking men had been trying to devise some way out of the tangle, some type of church which, though suited to the Scottish service, had a deeper spiritual meaning than those which were the fashion of the time. Perhaps the most influential of these seekers after better kirks was James Cooper (1846–1922), minister of the East Kirk, Aberdeen, and later Professor of Church History at Glasgow University. This learned and broad-minded scholar founded the Aberdeen Ecclesiological Society in 1886 which later became the Scottish Ecclesiological Society with centres in Edinburgh, Glasgow and Aberdeen. This Society still does useful work in drawing attention to the state of our churches and helped to bring about a great change for the better at the end of the 19th century.

However, it was not entirely the Scottish Ecclesiological Society which influenced the new outlook
towards churches, for the pendulum had begun to
swing before it was founded and its appearance was only
part of the movement, not the cause of it. The real
origins must be looked for as results of the English
movements earlier in the century, which have already
been discussed in this chapter, coupled with the fact that
the long tables were no longer required at communion
seasons.

What was more natural then than to follow the lead
of Anglicanism in the arrangement of Scottish churches?
However unwittingly it may have been done, that is
what happened, and a contributory factor was the
fashion for restoring medieval churches on what was
fondly imagined to be medieval lines.

At any rate the altar-like communion table was to
receive pride of place, it was set centrally at the end,
often the east end, of the church and a chancel built to
house it. As the minister celebrates from behind the
table it had to stand clear of the wall, but the general
impression given was that the Sacrament was celebrated
away from the people in a special sanctuary instead of
in their midst as the Reformers taught. This impression
is further heightened in some churches by the fact that
seats and stalls for a choir have often been placed between
the table and the congregation in emulation of the
misuse to which the Victorian Anglicans put the west
ends of their chancels. The pulpit was usually placed
on one side or other of the chancel arch, and, though
often much decorated, its importance was considerably
lessened, not only because of its siting but because the

dignified canopy of tradition was nearly always conspicuous by its absence.

The style of these churches was nearly always Gothic, but instead of borrowing all the motifs from south of the Border certain architects were studying more native styles, and the external results tended to become very much more pleasing and harmonised very much better with the scenery. Among the grander churches of this period are the Barony in Glasgow (1889), designed by Sir J. J. Burnett. It is a large church in pointed Gothic, with here and there details reminiscent of Dunblane Cathedral or Paisley Abbey; the interior is lofty and aspiring with a narrow chancel containing a table close to the wall on top of a flight of steps. Another great Gothic church is Govan (1888), designed by Sir Rowand Anderson, lined, as was his wont, with red brick. A classical church of the period is St. Cuthbert's, Edinburgh (1894), to the design of Hippolyte J. Blanc. Here the communion table is set in the chord of an apse with the elders' seats arranged round the wall after the manner of an ancient basilica. It has the choir stalls between the table and the people, but the arrangement of the apse was one which Professor Cooper recommended as being the best setting for the new type of plan in the Church of Scotland.

A much smaller church which is probably better known than those above mentioned is Crathie, Aberdeenshire. Its foundation stone was laid by Queen Victoria in 1893, and the architect, J. Marshall Mackenzie, made free use of typical Scottish detail. In plan it is cruciform with the table in an apse and one transept set aside for the use of the Royal Family. Another fine country church, erected in 1902 to take the place of an old one, is Inchinnan in Renfrewshire designed by Sir Rowand Anderson. Like Crathie it is a cruciform church, but the central tower, which was to have had a crowned termination, has never been finished.

By 1900 the average new parish church was a Gothic building, often with narrow side aisles flanking a broad nave, shallow transepts and a chancel containing the table. There were few excursions into any type of Renaissance architecture, though the admirable classic churches of Melrose and Coldstream, designed by J. M. Dick Peddie, seem better fitted for their purpose than their Gothic brethren.

A new influence, arising partly from the practical theories of Professor Cooper, with regard to the suitability of the reintroduction of the apse and partly from the Neo-Celtic cult of the time, was to produce a series of churches in what has been called a Scoto-Norman style designed by P. MacGregor Chalmers. These churches are a welcome relief from the rather fussy Gothic then current though their mannerisms tend to be slightly irritating. The general design is based on a simple, somewhat attenuated, Romanesque with an apse for the table and sometimes another smaller one at the end of an aisle for the font. When funds permitted, there is a tall tower based on the Dunning-Markinch tradition or the round Celtic Brechin-Abernethy type. Examples of Chalmers's work can be seen all over the country at St. Columba's, Elgin; Glasgow; St. Columba's, Blackhall; and St. Luke's, Edinburgh; Prestwick, Ardrossan; Carriden; St. Leonard's, Dunfermline; and St. Leonard's, St. Andrews. Rather unlike his usual very easily recognised style is St. Anne's, Corstorphine, with a simple Lombardic influence, but perhaps his best conceptions are the quite tiny churches at Achnacarry, Dervaig in Mull, with its round tower, and Hoselaw on the English border.

A particularly interesting church in Forfar, the Lowson Memorial, was designed in 1913 by J. Marshall Mackenzie. Had the First World War not intervened its general arrangements might well have become those accepted by the Church as long as Gothic architecture was in vogue. The table is placed in a spacious square chancel unencumbered with furniture, except the necessary seats for the elders round the walls. The organ and choir are accommodated on a wide screen at the west end of the nave. This church is a very fitting and inspiring example with which to close an era. The war of 1914 altered the whole aspect of church building socially and economically, hence it is desirable to outline the developments of the last forty years in a section of their own.

## CHAPTER VII

## POST-WAR CHURCHES: FULL CIRCLE?

THE twenty years between the wars was a difficult period for the Church. Large new housing areas and great districts of small bungalows sprang up on the outskirts of all the bigger towns, and unless churches could be quickly built in these places the tendency was for the inhabitants to drift into belonging to no church at all. The Home Board had therefore to take up the responsibility of providing religious buildings which besides a church had to include halls, kitchens, cloakrooms and all the paraphernalia of a social centre. This was not all: the ancient method of church maintenance by the heritors was abolished in 1925 and the upkeep of the churches of the old parishes was vested in the General Trustees of the Church, though, in practice, the responsibility rested with the individual Kirk Sessions. In 1929 occurred the reunion of the Establishment and the United Free Church. It has been mentioned that when the Free Church seceded in 1843 they were most active in building churches for themselves, so that before long most parishes in the country had at least two churches in which almost identical services were carried out. The large majority of these buildings are dull from an architectural point of view, though there are notable exceptions. In Glasgow the Free Church employed 'Greek' Thomson to design the famous

KINCARDINE-IN-MENTEITH, PERTHSHIRE

Gothic revival of 1816

ST. ANDREW'S, CLERMISTON, EDINBURGH

The contemporary idiom

churches at Caledonian Road (1858), St. Vincent Street (1859) and Queen's Park (1867). Then there was Thomas Pilkington who produced for them the striking, though near eccentric, Barclay Church in Edinburgh in 1862, and others equally curious in Kelso, Penicuik and Irvine. They also commissioned Charles Rennie Mackintosh's (1868–1922) only church, Queen's Cross in Glasgow, which was built in 1898. The main effect of the union of 1929 with regard to church building was that when one of the two ministers in a parish retired or died the congregations united under the remaining minister and normally chose one of the two churches to be the sole parish kirk. This was an admirable enough solution to the unpleasant division which formerly existed in every community in all respects, except that of the retention of our old churches. Several times in this short essay it has been mentioned that this or that church has been abandoned, generally interesting churches, or in the space available they could not have been mentioned. In many cases the reason for the old church being abandoned is that the combined congregation has chosen to worship in some 19th-century Free Church. There are numerous plausible reasons: the old kirk might be too far from the village, or it might require some renovation, and since there were no longer heritors to pester to do this the burden falls upon the congregation. Further, the ex-Free Kirk may have had a more recent installation of electric light or central heating, or perhaps even more comfortable pews!

Thus the repercussions of the Disruption on ancient churches are often nothing short of tragic. Many examples could be quoted, but enough to say that the cap will fit many congregations whose personal convenience has outweighed their sense of responsibility to the heritage of their country.

Occasionally, as in medieval and later days, the benefactions of some pious person have resulted in a church which can stand well above its contemporaries. Such is the Reid Memorial Church in Edinburgh designed by Leslie Grahame-Thomson in 1928. Here the Anglican tradition has been adopted, for it is long and narrow with a raised choir and the table still higher beyond. Though much of its detail is Scottish, the plan and arrangement owe little to Reformed tradition. But it is probably the last of the 'great' churches to be built, for in scale, size and elaboration it is equal to many of our medieval cathedrals.

The Church Extension buildings of this period, financed through the Home Board, are an interesting series. The conditions were roughly that a church seating about 500, a hall for about 300 and all the ancillaries thereof should be provided for a sum of £10,000. In some places an outside skin of stone was insisted upon and generally the style was a simple expression of some type of traditional architecture previous to Presbyterian Establishment, which was natural enough as the interiors were arranged on various pale versions of the inevitable Anglican plan.

These churches may be seen in most of the new housing areas around our greater towns. On the perimeter of Edinburgh is Stenhouse, designed by T. Aikman Swan; Saughton, by J. Inch Morrison; Granton Wardie, by Lorimer and Matthew; Craigentinny, by James Maclachlan; Craigmillar, by Reid and Forbes;

and Fairmilehead, by Leslie Grahame-Thomson. Among those around Glasgow are High Carntyne, by J. Taylor Thomson; King's Park, by Hutton and Taylor; Croftfoot, by Keppie and Henderson; and Gartcosh, by Gardner Maclean. At Dundee is Craigiebank, by Frank Thomson; and in Aberdeen, Hilton, by S. Bennet Mitchell; and Pittodrie, by A. G. R. Mackenzie. It may be noted that the Home Board was very catholic in its choice of architects so there is a considerable variety of treatment in dealing with approximately the same basic problem.

The difficult period following the Second World War (1939–45), with its severe imposition upon building and astronomical rise in building costs, has led to still greater retrenchment in church extension. The Ministry of Works allowed certain sums to be divided out between the churches of all denominations and the Church of Scotland could recommend, with the Ministry's permission, licences to build up to the sums agreed upon. This was an imposition hard enough to bear in itself, but the difficulty of the Home Board in raising funds was equally hard. The late Dr. John White pointed out that the average given for this purpose per head per year in certain districts amounted to the price of a packet of Woodbine cigarettes! However, in spite of that the Home Board is trying to keep up with the demands in the new housing areas to which the population is moving. Owing to building costs a church with attached hall can no longer be considered, and the maximum today is what is known as a hall-church or dual purpose building, which is in some ways a return to earlier days when the church was the only public building in a community and was liable to be used for purposes other than those strictly religious. As late as 1863 the General Assembly had to protest against churches being used for political meetings and social entertainments. So far has dual-purpose now been carried that the size of the main body of the kirk is built to suit the dimensions of a Badminton Court! The Anglican plan is still considered as the most suitable, which is understandable, for the table and other appointments of the sanctuary have to be in some sort of chancel which can be shut off from the nave or hall by folding doors or curtains when the remainder of the building is in use for secular purposes. A platform or stage is generally provided, and also the inevitable committee rooms, kitchen and cloakrooms. The need for these churches is very urgent, for many are planted in huge centres of population and serve areas the size of older towns which would contain a dozen places of worship. In most cases the site is of sufficient size to allow for a proper church being built in the future. When that is achieved the dual purpose structure will become the hall only.

So now it seems that the wheel has turned very nearly full circle: the screened chancel, granted part time and for a different reason, has returned; the nave, now hall, is used for every sort of parochial purpose; all is sliding back into the medieval plan. This is a sobering thought. Just where are we getting to? Back eight centuries, or forward on a pattern which happens to correspond in certain external ways with that so long ago? Perhaps there is much to be said for the integration of the life of the parish in one building catering for needs both

religious and social. It is the same with houses—the
'open' medieval plan is rapidly returning. Of course
the modern church or the modern house does not look
like the medieval ones in any respect, for the building
materials are so very different, but nevertheless the
basic planning for life in church and home is logically
getting around to an old well-tried pattern.

# INDEX OF PARISH CHURCHES
## MENTIONED IN THE TEXT

250

94